FROM GRASS
TO GARDENS

FROM GRASS TO GARDENS

How to Reap Bounty from a Small Yard

Janet Lembke

Illustrations by Joe Nutt

THE LYONS PRESS
Guilford, Connecticut
An imprint of The Globe Pequot Press

To buy books in quantity for corporate use
or incentives, call **(800) 962–0973, ext. 4551,**
or e-mail **premiums@GlobePequot.com.**

The Lyons Press is an imprint of The Globe Pequot Press.

10 9 8 7 6 5 4 3 2 1

Printed in the United States of America

Illustrations by Joe Nutt

Library of Congress Cataloging-in-Publication Data

Lembke, Janet.
    From grass to gardens : how to reap bounty from a small yard / Janet Lembke.
        p. cm.
    ISBN 1-59228-746-8
    1. Gardening. I. Title.
SB453L47 2006
635—dc22

2005027770

for Carroll,
who gardens, of course

✤ ACKNOWLEDGMENTS

It is a tradition among gardeners not to thank people who give us plants and seeds. Words, however, are a different matter, and several people merit my thanks for their help. Many are named in the book. Others, who should not be anonymous, are:

- Mary Ann Anderson, Master Gardener, who makes house calls
- Michael Goatley, turfgrass specialist at Virginia Tech, who contributed much information on the origins of Lawn
- Bess Nutt, friend forever, whose Green Man served as inspiration for the illustration
- Rhonda Sherman, vermiculturist at North Carolina State, who set me straight on worm-facts

Lilly Golden, my editor, also merits my gratitude for her loyal support.

CONTENTS

TOMATO HAVEN

> Tomatoes are good poetry.
>
> —*Rita Dove*

M Y YARD IS SMALL. IT'S A POSTAGE STAMP, A HAND-
kerchief, a mere suspicion of a yard. It's also urban, only
four blocks—past a private school, three churches, a
dozen houses, and a branch post office—from the downtown shopping district of the small community in which I live. And it answers
a wish that was formed more than two decades ago.

Tomato Haven—that's the role I envisioned for the yard that I
did not possess but certainly longed for in the late 1970s. I had access to a yard, all right. It was situated on a steep hill behind an
1840's house, adjacent to the basement apartment in which I lived.
With the landlord's permission, I did indeed dig a six-by-three-foot
tomato patch, hammered in support stakes, and set in the seedlings.
In mid-June, the tomatoes were as big as golf balls. By mid-July,
they'd become plump and started turning red. Soon, a crop! Soon,
the inimitable sweetness of a homegrown tomato! I harvested and
savored a few, but many of the fruits, both green and red, that I'd had
my eye on would go missing. The culprit was discovered one morning as it tried to haul a green tomato the size of a tennis ball up a
tree. Aha, squirrels were messing with my tomatoes, didn't matter if
the fruit was being used for food or toys. But it's hard to catch a

thievish squirrel, much less teach it some manners. As it happened, however, squirrels weren't the only snitchers. The landlord's wife complimented me on the fine homegrown flavor of the tomatoes in her backyard. If she'd asked for some, I'd have given them happily. As it was, I made a solemn vow to find a backyard of my own.

The search lasted from January through June of 1983. It took that long because I'd presented the real estate woman with criteria over and beyond finding a plot suitable for growing tomatoes. In this town of hills, it's not easy to find flattish yards. The yard also had to be amenable to being fenced so that my dog, an Australian shepherd, could go safely outside on her own. Then, I needed a front porch for sitting and sipping iced tea and reading in the summertime. More than that, front porch sitting is a time-honored Southern way of keeping track of neighborhood goings-on. And high ceilings inside the house were a must so that my large furniture, including an eight-foot-tall secretary inherited from my grandmother, could be accommodated. I also wanted to be close enough to the center of town to be able to walk there. Last, but not least, came price. Back then, I'd been divorced and on my own for four years. But, hallelujah, the town possessed many older fixer-uppers into which dog, large furniture, tomato dreams, and I might snuggle comfortably.

The town itself is worth a few words: Staunton, Virginia, founded by the Scotch-Irish in 1743 and situated in the center of the Shenandoah Valley. The Scotch-Irish are well known to be liars and drinkers, which means that you find good stories and much conviviality in our company. The British also sneaked in, building their Anglican churches within the limits of the town, so causing the Presbyterians to retreat to the countryside for worship. In the quirky British fashion that turns Cholmondeley into Chumley and Taliaferro into Tolliver, the name of the town is pronounced Stanton. The Blue Ridge Mountains are visible to the east, and to the west rises the long bony ridge of North Mountain. From some of Staunton's hilltops you can see them both. And Staunton, like Rome, was built on hills. Its precipitous streets resemble the ups and downs of a roller-coaster. The reason for covering the hills densely with private and public structures, from homes to stores, schools, theaters, the county courthouse, and City Hall, was that most of the people in the area farmed for a living, and farming was better conducted on gently rolling land than on steep hills.

The house that I found after the six-month search sits a third of the way up one of the steepest inclines, right at the point where it levels off for the space of three houses before resuming its up-ward sweep. The house is located in the Newtown Historic District, where many streets are named for greater and lesser presidents—Madison, Jefferson, Washington, Fillmore—and good-sized houses with their tiny yards stand cheek to jowl. The neighborhood boasts a virtual arboretum of native and exotic trees; among the former are southern catalpa, red and sugar maple, black walnut, hack-berry, dogwood, and Osage orange, while mimosa, ginkgo, and ailanthus represent foreign imports. Amid green shade in summer and intricately laced bare branches in winter, my house rests, a gray, white-trimmed frame dwelling with a tin roof and a four-columned porch that extends the entire width of the front. Down-stairs consists of four rooms and a bath—if you count the capacious foyer as a room. Three bedrooms, a bath, and a laundry room occupy the upstairs. Above that stands a full, undivided attic reached, when I bought the house, by a ladder placed underneath a trapdoor; the trapdoor has long since been replaced by pull-down steps.

Like that wooden trapdoor covering a square hole in the ceiling, much else had to be replaced, and that's one reason I was able to buy it for a song. The reason was that many of the houses, in this once sedately middle-class neighborhood of one-family homes, had been converted into apartments, many of which were rented by the clients of Social Services. Transience characterized the street, along with up-roar and almost daily visits by the police. The last twenty-plus years, however, have seen the onset of gentrification, started when a tum-bledown brick mansion just around the corner was renovated as a bed-and-breakfast. More and more houses have now reverted to one-family use.

But, oh, the house needed fixing. The wiring, for one, required drastic reworking. Not only was it old, but the system was not equipped to handle modern appliances. First of all, the slightest surge in power or the use of three lamps and a hair dryer at the same time would blow the fuses for an entire floor. In the early days, I had to plug my toaster oven via an extension cord into an upstairs outlet through a hole that existed for that very purpose. And the house had to be propped up, for it was sagging to the north. The undivided basement, accessible not from the house itself but from a door on the lower back porch, possesses the dimensions of the house proper. A cavernous place with a dirt floor and a twelve-foot-high ceiling, it's eminently suited for use as a dungeon or habitat for one's pet dragon. But steel columns, big around as telephone poles, were installed, and the listing of the house is at an end.

The enchantments, however, were, and still are, manifold. Take, to begin with, the two back porches, one up and one down, connected by stairs; as a result, two bedrooms have their own back doors. Then, little concave brass triangles—dust-catchers—deck the corners of the stairs, and a gingerbread arch, supported on either side by a stout wooden column, spans the wide entrance to the living room. The foyer is big enough to dance in, and so is the kitchen. Ballroom-style, I've danced in both. The dining room and one of the upstairs bedrooms each have a whole wall of bay windows. My grandmother's secretary looks handsome in the high-ceilinged living room, which is graced by its original chandelier. That extraordinary object looks like a large, upside-down, one-layer wedding cake, complete with white frosting and swathes of pink roses. Once upon a time, it and the ceiling fixtures throughout the house held gaslight.

Then, there was—and is—the yard. The lot itself is modest, only 43 by 125 feet. That's 5,375 square feet, a mere eighth of an acre. The house and a backyard shed occupy more than half of that space. In front the yard is minuscule and divided not quite down the center by a wide walk from sidewalk to porch steps. On the north side only three feet separate my house from the low concrete wall that marks the beginning of my uphill neighbor's yard. It's made of old-style concrete, full of rough chunks of limestone. On the south, eleven feet lie between the concrete wall bounding my yard and my downhill neighbor's wall. Once upon a time, the area was grassy, but it had been paved with asphalt before I laid eyes on the place. I'm one of only three people on the street with room to pull my car in beside the yard, and this was another of the lot's enchantments. Everyone else has to juggle and grab when it comes to parking spaces. Beyond the asphalt, grass leads into the backyard, which was constructed on two levels. The back lawns on either side of me rise steeply uphill, but when my house was built, someone had the wit to dig out most of the backyard; the upward tilt of the lower level is barely noticeable. The upper terrace, overgrown with honeysuckle when I bought the property, lies above a dry-built limestone wall and rises gently to another wall, half drywall, half old concrete. Each level is marked by a round cistern more than a yard in diameter; the city did not supply water to Newtown in its early days. And each level came with sturdy trees, a solitary black walnut below and, above, three specimens of something that I first identified as a slippery elm. But, more later about that mistaken ID.

One of the first projects after I moved in was collapsing the lower cistern, which yawned voraciously, threatening to swallow anyone, including the dog, who didn't pay attention to the lay of the land. I'd found a companion by then, and he arranged for several truckloads of topsoil to be hauled in as an antidote to red clay. He had a grand guy-time roaring about for an entire day on a rented Bobcat as he shoved the new dirt hither and yon before spreading it evenly. Predictably, grass seed was sown (I didn't know any better then). Then chain-link fencing was erected to contain our Australian shepherd, Towsie. She had a fine time in her yard, digging holes and responding to neighboring barks, and she also dispatched two 'possums and a groundhog. That last was a serious triumph, for groundhogs have very sharp teeth.

Another project was grubbing out the honeysuckle rampant on the terrace, but, as with the cistern, I was not the one who labored.

My elder son brought in his motorcycle club, and clad typically in beards, long hair, tattoos, and their riding colors, they spent a day uprooting vines, tilling the earth, and sowing grass seed. The price: all the soda and beer that they could drink.

When I acquired the house, I had no idea when it might have been built. The courthouse had no records, nor did the private foundation that keeps an eye on the city's architecture. Conjecture zeroed in on the turn of the century, 1899 to 1900. Then, eight years after moving in, I learned the precise answer in a surprising way. At that time I was spending spring and summer in the boonies of North Carolina with my companion who had become my husband, the Chief, a retired Navy man, but I often came north during those months for appointments with doctors and dentists or to tend to the needs of my ailing mother. During one brief trip, I began a dash out the front door for whatever errand was summoning me. The dash ended almost instantly, for there on my front porch stood two women, one tiny and elderly, the other taller and middle-aged, who asked if they might come in. They turned out to be mother and daughter, and the younger woman was taking her mother to visit all the places in which she'd lived during a long, long life. Of course they were invited inside, and of course we talked. Her father, Simon Early, had built the house in 1910, when she, Racheal, was seven years old. (Yes, that's the proper spelling of her name.) And that was the year that she and her parents moved in. Two of her brothers were born in the house. Though she was well into her eighties, she traipsed upstairs and down. I learned that the house had always had indoor baths, one on each floor. And my upstairs laundry room had, in its original incarnation, served as the nursery. Her father, Mr. Early, had lived in the house until he died in 1949.

"Oh, I remember, I remember," she said, smiling. "It's much the same. Would you like to see pictures?"

Silly question. The old photographs showed the family, dignified father clad in suit and tie, gracious mother wearing a long lawn dress, Racheal in ruffles, and the three boys in knickers. One photo displayed the upside-down wedding cake chandelier. I learned about the yard, too. Mrs. Early had kept two milk cows in back of the house. And the concrete wall up on the terrace had once been part of a livery stable, accessible by an alley that still exists.

It was at least five years after this encounter that we found the handwriting on the wall. That may sound dire, but it was not. Why it had never come to notice before is baffling. I think it was the Chief who spotted it—a fine example of Palmer penmanship gracefully inscribed in the plaster beside one of the wooden columns supporting the gingerbread arch. It reads:

> *August 18th*   *19*
> *first*   *100 -*
> *hundred*   *- - - - - - - -*
>   *Chas. E. Early*

The meaning remains a mystery. Charles—a son, most likely—making much of his first earnings? Brought home on August 18, 1919? I'll never know, but the words connect me with a stirring sweetness to the lives lived in this house.

Tomato Haven was not established in 1983, the year that I moved in, for the month was August, and other tasks were at hand— unpacking boxes, arranging furniture, putting white paint over the hot pink that some misguided soul had used on the shelves of the dining room's built-in breakfront, and, a short six weeks after moving in, falling terminally in love with the Chief. The only planting accomplished in 1983 was that of a climbing 'Blaze' rose, which the Chief purchased at a supermarket for $1.98 and installed on the south side of the front yard. Trunk now as big around as my wrist, it is still gloriously in place—gray house, white pillars, red roses. But as soon as May arrived the following year, the Chief and I were both out there removing grass and digging up a tomato patch on the yard's north side. The south side was out of the question, for it supported a mammoth black walnut tree, probably a volunteer from a nut planted by a squirrel. *Juglans nigra* is notoriously unfriendly to any other kind of greenery that tries to gain a foothold near it. The reason is that the roots secrete a toxic substance, juglone, that poisons other vegetation. The tree had most successfully done in any competitors. The soil beneath it was bare, except for a few furtive patches of ground ivy.

But the north side offered space for a garden. Thank goodness for male muscle! The job of breaking ground would have taken me weeks, for grass has stick-tight roots and the earth here is full of stones, ranging in size from peach pit to brick. But the Chief manned spade, shovel, hoe, and rake with unflagging vigor, and the tomato patch was created in a few days. In its creation, we sometimes felt like archaeologists, for the earth yielded all sorts of artifacts from days gone by—the rusted head of a rake, several marbles, bits of broken blue-and-white china, a doll's porcelain arm, and an old key—the kind with an oval handle, a long stem, and a bit at the end. Eight 'Big Boy' tomatoes were planted in the newly turned earth, and, not being able to leave well enough alone, we also put in four 'California Wonder' bell peppers.

Earth responded generously. No fertilizer had been applied, but the tomatoes grew fruit bigger than softballs, and the pepper plants not only provided peppers far larger than any I've ever seen in a supermarket but also developed woody stems more than an inch in diameter. It was as if the soil on our yard's north side had become tired of grass, grass, grass, and nothing but grass. We gathered the bounty and rejoiced.

The Chief also cut down that killer black walnut. And at the picnic after our July wedding in 1984, some of the guests used the massive trunk as a bench. Later, because black walnut provides a highly desirable wood for cabinetry, we tried to sell the trunk to a local buyer of timber, who turned it down on the grounds (unlikely we thought) that someone might have driven large nails or a spike into it, either of which would damage sawmill blades. The trunk and stouter limbs didn't languish long in the yard, though.

The man who made house calls to repair my increasingly cranky IBM typewriter asked what we planned to do with umpty board feet of black walnut. I shrugged. Did he know of anyone who might want it? Yes, his father, a retiree obsessed by woodcarving. The repairman sawed the trunk into shorter lengths and carted it off. Several weeks later, we were presented with the gleaming figure of a small black bear.

I couldn't have known it then, of course, but the felling of the walnut and the subsequent drenching of the yard in sunlight were the first omens that the yard had vast potential to become something more than just Tomato Haven. It could be Total Garden. But we spent the next eighteen springs and summers fishing and growing vegetables in North Carolina. Towsie went with us; after she died, we were accompanied by our Doberman, Sally, now forever in the Carolina earth. The opportunity for conversion did not arise.

THE GRASS
EXTERMINATION
PROJECT

And, as it works, th' industrious bee
Computes its time as well as we.
How could such sweet and
wholesome hours
Be reckon'd, but with herbs
and flowers!

—*Andrew Marvell,*
"Thoughts in a Garden"

I'VE GARDENED ALL OF MY ADULT LIFE—FLOWERS, vegetables, shrubs. Touching earth, sowing seeds, planting seedlings, getting my hands dirty and my body sweaty have always been a source of intense pleasure. To watch a seed sprout and grow, to harvest and taste earth's bounty is to partake of a recurring miracle. And, as Shirley Hibbard, a gardener and wise woman, said in 1877, "Contact with the brown earth cures all diseases." Diseases—bleak, painful absences of ease—include those of the spirit as well as those of the body. So, to garden is also to find both high-flying joy and a solace for sorrow. It is a means of healing. And, after eighteen years of marriage, I needed healing after the Chief died early in the spring of 2002. But before he made his last journey, we had indulged in our usual garden dreaming, the seeds that he'd ordered had arrived, and the least I could do was plant them. To watch them sprout and grow would be a sort of resurrection.

11

For every one of our eighteen years together, we'd worked vegetable gardens—or rather, he tilled, planted, and picked, while I picked and preserved. He loved both the labor and its results, and I held back, putting in flowers but letting him lord it over tomatoes, beans, squash, and a colorful, savory host of others. One garden soon became two, and each expanded every year until we were raising veggies on 5,000 square feet. That's not just a vegetable patch; it's a truck garden. We gave produce to friends, neighbors, the mail carrier, the UPS man, and the FedEx woman. But in the Chief's last few years, illness robbed him of strength. So, each spring he would arrange for a man to turn the soil thoroughly with our heavy tiller. Then, from start to finish, I would make the crop. The task became easy when the Chief presented me with a mini-tiller, a little twenty-pound machine that purred up and down the aisles between the rows. We'd never had a cleaner garden. But the Carolina days came to an end the March that he died. I chose then to live full-time in the town of my growing up and in the gray frame house where he had died and in back of which we'd once established Tomato Haven.

But the patch in which we'd grown those supernally large tomatoes and peppers no longer existed. Grass and weeds had long since commandeered bare earth. Clearly, if I wanted homegrown tomatoes without having to make a trip to one of the local farmers' markets, I'd have to get rid of some grass. Some grass? Why not all of the grass? A neighbor borrowed a heavy-duty tiller and churned up the strip that had once been and would again be Tomato Haven. I set to work on the front yard myself. From yard to garden—that was the aim.

Yard and garden—both words come from the Old High German *gart*, which referred to a small enclosed, sometimes paved space beside a dwelling. It was an unembellished outdoor extension of the house. Somewhere along the way, garden entered the picture—an ornamented yard, an area lush with greenery and flowers, a place productive of fruits and vegetables, a haven for the spirit. I thought, Out with the yard! In with gardens front and back!

All our garden tools had been brought north—everything from the mini-tiller to hoes, shovels, and dandelion-digger, as well as a wooden glider to perch on when my back and knees had had enough of labors. And that leads me to an important garden precept:

Seating arrangements—chairs, benches, gliders— suit a garden, be they for resting, sitting to read, bird-watching, or lazing in the evening to admire fireflies.

The five-gallon buckets that used to hold drywall compound—those buckets that we filled, sometimes two at a time, with Carolina tomatoes—came north, too, along with my lightweight three-legged stool. So, gloved, sitting upon my tripod, and wielding a short-handled hoe, I began work on the front yard in April of 2002. The goal on pleasant days was one five-gallon bucket of extracted turf. The green stuff on the north side of the yard, including weeds, was completely grubbed up that first year, and so was some on the south side, for I'd brought plants from Carolina, too—sunny yellow irises (*Iris* species), lemon yellow and double orange daylilies (*Hemerocallis*), a yellow-flowered sedum, double coreopsis (*Coreopsis grandiflora*), oregano (*Origanum vulgare*), and beargrass (*Yucca filamentosa*), which is sometimes called Adam's thread and needle because of the leaves' sharp terminal points and the little white filaments that curl outward along their edges.

Those plants from Carolina are living links between Then and Now. They are an umbilical cord through which the Past sustains and nourishes the Present.

The following year, the grass on the front yard's south side had been totally exterminated. Part of it is now a cucumber patch in the summer and a cole-crop patch in the fall. My journal records the first bright yellow cuke blossoms in early June, the first fruit three weeks later. The variety is one called 'Little Leaf', and its leaves are tiny indeed—I can conceal one with my palm. The cukes (*Cucumis sativa*) are short and plump, a variety suited to pickling, but those in my garden are mostly destined for the refillable pot that stays all summer long in the refrigerator—cukes and onions sliced razor-thin and marinated in equal parts of vinegar and water. Those that escape the refrigerator pot will go into salads or be given to family members, friends, and even passersby.

Why cucumbers in the front yard? Because they don't thrive in the backyard vegetable patch, where they were planted late in the first spring of my full-time return to Staunton, but I'll give the reason for that later. Nor are the cukes the only plants in front. They occupy a middle ground encircled not only by the Carolina transplants and the climbing 'Blaze' rose (*Rosa x odorata*) that the Chief put in more than two decades ago but also by newly acquired golden and peach-colored daylilies, 'Patriot' plantain lilies (*Hosta fortunei*) with green and white variegated leaves, tickseed (*Coreopsis verticillata*) with ferny leaves, fiendishly bright blanket flowers of the variety known as 'Goblin' (*Gaillardia aristata*), sweet peppers (*Capsicum annuum*), and one so-called "cowhorn" pepper (*C. annuum*), which develops a slender, curved fruit ten inches long. That pepper is actually a variety of cayenne, with considerable heat—30,000 units—on the Scoville scale. It turns riotously red.

No vegetables grow on the north side. That territory is divided among four tribes. One is perennial flowers—irises, columbine (*Aquilegia x hybrida*), black-eyed Susan (*Rudbeckia hirta*), dusty miller (*Centaurea cineraria*), and more blanket flowers. In their company are several summer snowflakes (*Leucojum aestivum*), which almost met doom. We had transplanted them from North Carolina in the 1980s but were never in Staunton during their spring bloom-time, and every year they were mowed down before they flowered. But some long-concealed vitality emerged in the second spring of my return to Tomato Haven: leaves rose, stalks emerged, and sprouted buds that opened into small, nodding white bells with faint green stripes. The second tribe on the north side consists of sedums and sempervivums, some green or silvery gray (*Sedum cauticolum* and others), some with bloodred edges on their dark green leaves (*Sedum spurium*, also called 'Dragon's Blood'); they flower pink, rose, and yellow. The third tribe is that of perennial herbs—oregano (*O. vulgare*), thyme (*Thymus vulgaris*), winter savory (*Satureja montana*), tarragon (*Artemesia dracunculus*), chives (*Allium schoenoprasum*), creeping rosemary (*Rosmarinus officinalis*), and sage (*Salvia officinalis*). The fourth tribe, that of treekind, is represented by a single miniature species of Japanese origin, *Acer palmatum dissectum*, which means "deeply cut palmate maple." The label placed on it in the nursery also gives it the common name of 'Crimson Queen Laceleaf Maple', and its delicate, deeply incised little leaves show crimson in the spring with dark green emerging as summer comes in, though the lacy foliage on new twiglets is totally crimson. The red color protects new leaves from being burnt by the sun. Nor are maples the only trees that use this color to ward off harm; the new leaves of redbud (*Cercis canadensis*), for one, are scarlet. And, fly over a jungle, you may see much red in the canopy. Autumn turns the little maple's leaves bright red, and with the first black frost, they flutter to the ground in a single night. I have been fussed at by a professor, who teaches botany at the local college, for planting a nonnative species. But the yard is small—only a tiny tree suits it, and the maple is quite at home amid the herbs, not one of which, except for tarragon, is native to the New World. (The backyard, where extermination is still underway, is chock-full of aliens—dandelions, common mallows, ground ivy, honeysuckle, and others, many of which were imported intentionally by early settlers.) Yearly, a few annuals join the front yard's motley company—zinnias (*Zinnia elegans* and *Z. hybrida*) and petite marigolds (*Tagetes patula*) housed in a one-by-three-foot wooden planter. With the blanket flowers, they provide gaudy color—a soft explosion of yellow, red, pink, and orange—until the first hard frost strikes.

How do I chose plants for the front yard? Partly because the color of a particular flower or leaf enchants. Partly because experience tells me that certain varieties are sure to grow. But with something new, something totally untried, a precept is at work:

> *Know your plant-hardiness zone and know, as well, what a plant needs in the way of soil and sunshine. Good catalogues will give all the information that you require, but also consult your gardening friends. Inquire, too, at local garden centers—not the super-stores that also carry plants in season—but with people intimately familiar with your area.*

So that I can tread lightly among the plants without stepping on any (save the thyme that's wonderfully fragrant when it's crushed), rose-colored hexagonal pavers make a gently winding path from the front walk to the cold frame on the yard's north side. Nor are pavers the only places to put my feet. Flatter pieces of native limestone, dug up as I cleared away the grass, fill in some corners. And when I first attempted to excavate a hole for the little maple, I discovered a most peculiar object—a metal box, its six-by-three-inch top stamped with a W in the center of a circle formed by the words, "Dayton Supply, Dayton, O." It was the successor to the cisterns in back—a primitive sort of meter, installed when the city's mains began delivering water to Newtown. Goodness only knows how long it's been out of use, but it does mark the site of the present waterline—not a good place to try planting a tree, even a tiny one. Surrounded by pavers, the meter is back in use now as part of the path—which leads me to a precept:

> *Gardens deserve paths, be they winding or straight. And paths may be made of many materials, from*

stone through metal to bioglop, the last being a com-
bination of inorganic and organic materials—Port-
land cement, sand, peat moss, and water—that can
be formed into whatever shapes the maker desires.
Paths may even be grassy. Their purpose is to help
feet step between the plants, not on them.

The two-level backyard is still striving for a grassless state, with
half of its lower level now cleared. Fruit-bearing pear trees (*Pyrus
communis*) have been installed there, and a Norway spruce (*Picea
abies*), once a four-foot Tannenbaum decked with tinsel, lights, and
ornaments, now towers taller than my three-story house. I've put in
red currant bushes (*Ribes rubrum*), as well, and made two sizeable
vegetable patches. The lower backyard also includes some shrubs—
bridal wreath (*Spiraea x prunifolia*) and rose-of-Sharon (*Hibiscus
syriacus*)—that came with the house back in 1983 and were surely
planted long before that. The upper level, a terrace shaded by what I'd
thought were slippery elms, still retains much weedy grass, but that
kind of green stuff is on its way out, at least in imagination. 'King Alfred' daffodils (*Narcissus pseudonarcissus*), descended from daffs
grown in North Carolina by the Chief's father in the 1930s, have for
years made a flourish of golden trumpets in the spring. (Note to the
professor of botany: daffodils are an introduced species.) The daffs
have recently been joined by azaleas 'Elsie Lee', a cultivar loaded with
lavender blossoms, and 'Hilda Niblett', notable for bearing peach-
colored flowers and white ones on the same bush. And one fern
(species unknown) already unfurls its green grace up there; it was given
by a woman who was ripping ferns out of a shady flower border beside
her house on the grounds that they were as pushy as weeds. Mind's eye
revels in visions of more azaleas adding their blossom-light to the
terrace in spring, and more ferns uncoiling their cool green fronds.

As for those putative slippery elms, it took twenty years for me to
learn their true identity. A friend, who had brought perennial flowers

from her garden to set in mine, said, "Oh, you have hackberries!" And so I do—*Celtis occidentalis*. To my credit, it *is* a member of the Elm family. To my discredit I should have recognized it, for a Carolina neighbor had a huge specimen in his yard, but he didn't call it "hackberry." He called it "warty bark." And that aptly describes the protuberant bumps on its trunk and limbs.

As I've said, the open space surrounding my house is not much bigger than a postage stamp, and this smallness makes it manageable. The entire front yard, not including the walk, contains fewer than 260 square feet. The lower level in back has the greatest area at about 2,000 square feet, while the shady upper level accounts for just over 400 square feet. The whole, some 2,660 square feet of arable land in all, is only half the size of our North Carolina truck garden.

I can handle that. Out with the grass!

Why should I desire ardently to exterminate the grass? Whence came this itch, the only cure for which is to grub the green blades out by their stubborn little roots and put in all else? Every other front and backyard on the street has a lawn—as did my yard, once upon a time. Most also are decked with trees and shrubs, and some have gardens—irises, lilies, salvia, chrysanthemums—along with the grass. Most of the yards in town are similar, though a few have indulged in Total Gardens, especially in the front yards that occupy steep, hard-to-mow banks in this hilly town. But isn't grass easier to care for than gardens? Yes, and then again, no. Yes, if it's allowed to grow like Topsy and include lots of weeds: all that's needed then is an occasional pass with the lawn mower. Most of the lawns on my street fall into this category; they are abundantly green, but much of that verdant color comes from weeds like plantain, wild violets, and the inevitable dandelions. But no, they are not easier to care for if perfection is insisted on: grass and nothing but grass. That makes for a monoculture, and monocultures, be they lawns or timber-company pine plantations, are blinkered, single-minded places, in which habitats are lost and chemicals—herbicides, pesticides, fertilizers—must be used to maintain the status quo.

I grubbed out grass and wondered about the human yen for green. Where does the idea of Lawn come from? Where, its practice and seemingly endless expanses? So, I started grubbing for answers, too, checking into various views of Lawn and into theories of why it exists. My New Hampshire cousin, Bess, proprietor of a ten-acre hayfield and an unassuming patch of grass around her house, cut respectively by a local farmer and a landscaping company, says, "To sell lawn mowers, that's what grass is for. Oh, and if you have kids, to play ball on." And naturalist David Quammen, in an essay called "Rethinking the Lawn," writes of his certainty, in his teenaged days, that lawns were dreamed up by the Communists to keep suburban youngsters in America from giving their energies to tasks more thrilling than mowing vast acres of greensward; in his view, riding a lawn mower was a devious way of diverting thought from riding Sputnik into outer space. In his later years, he recanted for a while and maintained a standard swath of grass. But today, his tools a hammock and a copy of *Leaves of Grass*, he favors a yard that's gone native and turned into meadow.

Lawn is a more serious matter, of course, than these two commentators might indicate. Grass itself, in many varieties, has been around for some seventy million years. Lawn consists of grass, of course, but it's made of rigorously selected varieties and is called "turfgrass" by the specialists. That redundant word—"turf" alone would do—was coined in the twentieth century by the landscaping industry to differentiate the stuff from other members of the Graminiae, the Grain family, which includes food crops like wheat and maize that are usually planted in fields, not yards and parks. Areas devoted to grass have been around for millennia but morphed into Lawn as we know it today only about three hundred years ago, a mere blip of time in the uncountable eons that have passed since the planet cooled and its chemistry made life possible. Once upon a fairly recent time, "lawn" referred to untilled ground, a glade in the woods, or a pasture. "Lawn" in its modern sense of a piece of soil intentionally planted with grass and closely mowed did not appear in the English language until 1733, when the *Gardeners Dictionary*, written by one Mr. Miller, said this: "*Lawn* is a great Plain in a Park, or a spacious Plain adjoining to a noble Seat. . . . As to the Situation of a Lawn, it will be best in the Front of the House, and to be open to the neighboring Country and not pent up with Trees."

The first incident that prefigured the making of the modern Lawn occurred about fourteen thousand years ago when humankind clambered out of its biologically ordained hunting-gathering niche by learning to domesticate plants and animals. Grass had always been part of the human experience, but the new era of farming meant that people, not grass, were in control. Neanderthals and Cro-Magnons, however, didn't plant lawns, although they may have had something similar, but not for aesthetic or recreational reasons. What they had was something that later developed into the village green, a special place where domesticated animals could graze close to human habitation (no one wanted to go running through the woods to look for them). A text on turfgrass science says, "This grazing system was an act of survival for both the man and his animals. The closely cropped grass became a symbol which exists today as a basis for landscaping around homes, businesses, in parks, and other places of beauty. It also served as a playground for young and old." (Child, wash off your feet before you dare enter this house.) But despite the well-mowed look of a village green, it took a prodigiously long time for us to realize that we ran the show when it came to this green stuff that we don't eat because, unlike cows, sheep, deer, and giraffes—ruminants with quadripartite stomachs—we can't digest it.

As might be guessed from Mr. Miller's pronouncements on the subject, it was the British, famed far and wide for their eccentricity, who not only thought up the notion of Lawn but also designed and planted acres of what we today would easily recognize as the Real Thing. It developed as a firm rejection of continental gardens, which were planned not by landscapers but the very architects who built mansions and palaces. The idea was that a garden should be an outdoor extension of a building, complete with rooms and entryways, and the organizing principle was a geometric symmetry. Lines were straight, and patterns dominated the designs. Thus, we have the term "landscape architecture," although "architecture" actually refers to expert building and, in particular, to carpentry (note, please, that we never speak of landscape carpentry). Lawn as we know it came about when William Kent, an English painter and architect, was seized by a revolutionary fit, by an urge to relax rigidly formal arrangements. He proceeded to create a parklike garden of great irregularity—meandering brook, curving paths, trees and shrubs left in their natural shapes, and, not least, lots of grass—for the Earl of Burlington in 1734. The grass was separated from the natural world beyond by a ha-ha, a sunken ditch. And how did a ditch gain such a peculiar name? A 1712 translation of a French book on gardening explains: "Thorough-Views, call'd *Ah, Ah,* . . . are Openings . . . to the very Level of the Walks, with a large and deep Ditch at the Foot . . . which surprises . . . and makes one cry, *Ah! Ah*! from whence it takes its Name." Nor was use of the ha-ha restricted to the environs of the wealthy in Europe, no indeed. George Washington's parklike sward at Mount Vernon was enclosed by just such a ditch.

But Lawn still hadn't made its full appearance. Blame Lancelot "Capability" Brown (1715–1783) for wishing it upon the world. In his day, the English nobility had a passion for planting vast forested parks, the avenues of which were seen as extensions of garden paths. Capability, so nicknamed for his frequently made remark that a place had "capabilities of improvement," came up with the concept of a natural landscape that would blur the boundaries of garden and park. The typical Brownian design featured trees set alone or in small clusters, bodies of water with unpatterned contours, and, of course, grass in vast sweeps that followed the lay of the land. The grounds of Blenheim Palace, built in the early 1700s and the birthplace of Winston Churchill, were originally laid out in the extravagantly formal style of Versailles, but by midcentury, Capability had reworked them to suit his taste for informality. Nonetheless, Lawn didn't catch on right then as a popular phenomenon, for the grass had to be cut by men wielding scythes. Blenheim, for example, needed a crew of fifty to keep the grass pleasingly short. And their scythes had to be exceedingly sharp so that the grass was actually cut, not just bent over. Then, after they had done their job, the lawn women came in to remove the shorn grass. Lawn was altogether an expensive proposition. Common people made do with cottage gardens.

Enter Edwin Beard Budding (c. 1795–1846), a machine foreman in a cloth mill located in Stroud, Gloucestershire. It was he who put Lawn within the reach of ordinary folks when he invented the push mower. Working with the mill's nap-cutting machines, he noted that the principles of their bladed reels could be transferred to a mechanism that could whack grass down to a respectable height. On May 18, 1830, he received a patent and went into partnership with John Ferrabee, a foundry owner, to make machines "for the purpose of cropping or shearing the vegetable surface of lawns, grass plats, and pleasure grounds." It was a clunky device, made completely of cast iron, and its operation must have required considerable muscle— man's work, not woman's. But it did the job, with cast-iron gear-wheels sending power from the rear roller to the cutting reel. Not long after, side-wheel mowers came along, and by 1900, some mowers had been fitted out with gasoline-powered engines. Today, the aficionados of old lawn mowers have even formed clubs to exhibit antique models and share their lore.

The invention of such a handy-dandy grass-cutting tool brought a noticeable burgeoning of Lawn in Britain and America. The British mania for grass is well-expressed by the poet Gordon Bottomley (1874–1948) in "To Ironmongers and Others." Granted, he was rhyming specifically against the pollution caused by heavy industry, but he also speaks to a general notion that England deserves grass:

> When you destroy a blade of grass
> You poison England at her roots.
> Remember no man's foot can pass
> Where evermore no green life shoots.

It was shortly after the Civil War that the U.S. was overcome by an equal mania. Front Lawns became all the rage, for they not only made an aesthetic statement but also proclaimed that the people who carpeted their front yards with grass had made it successfully into the ranks of the middle class. Nor were homeowners the only ones who surrounded themselves with turfgrass. Turf planted on purpose is found in commercial venues, parks, golf courses, and sundry other recreational facilities like ballparks and football fields. It also grows abundant on roadsides and median strips. Acre on acre, it is found in cemeteries. The first airport in the United States, located in College Park, Maryland, had turf runways. In fact, turf was the only covering for runways until planes became so large and heavy that they ruined the live surface.

Ironically, the grasses used for turf are as exotic as my miniature Japanese laceleaf maple: not one of them is native to the Americas. Kentucky bluegrass, *Poa pratensis,* "grass of the meadows," originated either in Europe or the Middle East, though it had become well established in England by the eighteenth century. The source of Bermuda grass, *Cynodon dactylon,* "fingerlike dogtooth" (for the sheathed runners), is Africa. Why foreign grasses? In the first place, the seeds were imported because American grasses were too fragile to withstand grazing by the livestock brought here by colonists. Then, exotic species could be fiddled with by specialists, often handsomely sponsored by the United States Department of Agriculture, to create an ideal Lawn, thick and green and suited to a variety of climates. Lawn could stretch across the country from cool New England through the humid South and all the way to the arid deserts of the West.

The game of golf, which originated in Scotland in the 1400s, was undoubtedly a large factor behind the transformation of great expanses of shaggy landscape into neatly trimmed greensward. But in its earliest incarnation, golf was a seaside sport played on the east coast of the Kingdom of Fife. The players used sticks or clubs—not golf clubs with heads but rather clubs like truncheons—to whack pebbles over a course abounding in natural hazards, like sand dunes and rabbit warrens. The objective was to put the pebble in a hole with the least possible number of whacks. The rough was known from the beginning, but not fairways and greens. But as it happened, the notable Royal and Ancient Golf Club of Saint Andrews came into being right at the time that Capability Brown had reinvented the landscapes surrounding stately homes. Then, after Mr. Budding's lawn mower had made maintenance easy, golf courses that we would recognize as such appeared far and wide.

Lawn: an estimate made in 1996 puts its acreage in the United States alone, be it on a golf course or a yard or beside a highway, at a conservative 48 million acres. But the population certainly did not stop increasing its numbers at that time, and with growth in the number of people who have set new homes in a sea of green, there's been a concomitant increase in the area covered by turfgrass. Some of that acreage, though not yet much of it, is now being covered with a relatively new product called Grasspave, which is a porous structure planted with grass and capable of bearing the weight of a tractor-trailer truck without crushing the tender green stuff. It's used in places like parking lots as an alternative to asphalt—not a bad idea, for grass keeps surface temperatures down and allows for the filtration of surface water.

But, 48 million acres of Lawn! How did this happen? The historian Virginia Scott Jenkins puts it this way: "Advertising, mass marketing, the democratization of golf, the influence of popular magazines, the upheaval of two world wars, and the growth of the lawn industry in the twentieth century introduced lawns to large segments of the American public. The lawn industry has developed into a powerful vested interest in the continuing and expanding culture of grass." And the industry has been supported without stint by the likes of the USDA, the United States Golf Association, and the people next door.

Forty-eight million acres of Lawn—that's downright boggling. It's more than the acreage of all New England, plus Maryland and Delaware. And think of all the care that Lawn demands! Seeds; rolls of sod; tools like hoes, rollers, and sprinklers; fertilizers; pesticides and herbicides; landscaping contractors; lawn maintenance firms; not to mention mowers and weed whackers and the fuel that they consume—Virginia alone spent more than 2.5 *billion* dollars in 1998 on just the equipment needed to maintain turf, and in that year, the value of unpaid, Do-It-Yourself grass-care exceeded one billion dollars (think on that, David Quammen). According to Bruce Butterfield, the National Gardening Association's Research Director, the DIY figure in the U.S. for 2003 was 10.4 billion dollars. There are 84 million households in this country, and fully 78 percent of them were engaged one way or another in yard care during that year. The average expenditure per household came to $1,267 (a family could vacation on that!). And in 2003, lawn-care professionals, from landscape architects to the local TruGreen ChemLawn franchise, did 31.3 billion dollars' worth of business. Add that to the DIY figure: 41.7 billion dollars. That comes to 5.7 billion dollars more than the Gross State Products of North and South Dakota combined. It's 16 billion dollars more than China admits to budgeting for its People's Liberation Army. It's as near as makes no never mind to the annual Gross Domestic Product of New Zealand.

Out with the grass, in with all else. I'm in the camp of Andrew Marvell (1621–1678), who lived before Lawn reared its little green blades. As Marvell did in "Thoughts in a Garden," I want to be "stumbling on melons, as I pass, and ensnared with flowers." So, in my yard I'm exterminating grass and behaving as if it were of no use whatsoever except to generate income for the people who make products to create and maintain Lawn. But grass has its virtues, of course. One, mentioned above, is that places surrounded by greenery of any kind are cooler than places surrounded by asphalt. More important, for a world concerned about the ways in which global warming may alter climate systems, the greenhouse gases, significantly including carbon dioxide, have been cited as villains. But vegetation, taking in carbon dioxide and releasing oxygen, reverses the human breathing system. Forests, gardens, and grass act as carbon sinks—places, that is, in which carbon is sopped up and stored for long periods of time. Trees sequester more CO_2 than other vegetation, but any green-growing plant, even a weed, is capable of storing it. An article that appeared in 2002 estimates that regularly mowed turfgrass in golf-course fairways and putting greens is capable of storing 12 to 15 million tons of

carbon annually during the next twenty-five to thirty years. Naturally, plants don't keep it locked up forever. Some of the circum-
stances in which it's released include the felling or natural decay of a
tree and the disturbance of soil and root systems.

So, when I use my hoe or tiller to turn over the vegetable patch in
my backyard, I'm releasing carbon, albeit in minuscule quantities. But
hoeing and tilling are hardly irresponsible practices: they ready the soil
for more plants, and more plants mean more storage of carbon. And
I've learned that a garden need not go bare all winter long or, worse,
wear an overcoat of weeds, but may be used for growing a cover crop
like rye that gets tilled back into the earth come spring. In summer, the
soil benefits from green manure, a neatly sassy term for plants that
provide ground cover and so shade out weeds or, like beans and other
legumes, fix nitrogen in the soil. They sequester carbon, as well.

But back to the virtues of small blades of green. James B. Beard,
a scientist with a vested appreciation of turfgrass, sings its praises
wholeheartedly and divides its benefits to humankind into three cat-
egories: functional, recreational, and aesthetic. The first includes its
abilities not only to dissipate heat and sequester carbon but also to
prevent soil erosion, keep down dust, reduce glare and noise, and
keep nuisance animals at bay. A closely mowed lawn has no hidey-
holes for groundhogs, skunks, and cottontails, it wards off snakes,
and it does not furnish food to urbanized deer. The main recreational benefit is that turf provides low-cost surfaces for sports like
baseball, football, tennis, lacrosse, croquet, bowls, and horseshoes.
Thus, in Dr. Beard's view, our physical and mental health is en-
hanced, and if we don't take part in grassy games but merely watch,
we benefit from being entertained. As for the aesthetic aspects of
Lawn, he reports that it not only complements its neighboring trees
and shrubs but also offers beauty in itself, which in turn enhances
"quality of life, mental health, social harmony, community pride,
and increased property values."

It's not possible to disagree with all these points, though I have
serious reservations about a few. There's a minor quibble, too: Dr.
Beard fails to say a word about the fact that a blade of grass can act

as a reed if it's placed between the carpal and first joints of the thumbs—blow and a piercing whistle will split the air. My first real quarrel has to do with noise abatement. It's true, as Dr. Beard says, that "turfgrass surfaces absorb harsh sounds significantly better than hard surfaces such as pavement, gravel, or bare ground." But note that he totally overlooks the roar of the mowing machine, not to mention the fact that gardens also lessen noise, whether it comes from traffic, neighbors talking, and the loud music playing next door. My main reservation—no, my total disagreement with one of Beard's views—has to do with the beauty of Lawn. Yes, green blades of tidy, close-cut grass lend freshness to a landscape. Yes, it's lovely to look at. It's been proposed that we also may have a biological yen for grass that's been hard-wired into us ever since we got up on our hind legs and walked. And where did we first try out our new bipedal gait? On an African savanna, an open grassland, the kind of place in which we could readily see if any dangerous animal (including our own kind) was stalking us. Because we evolved to walk on a grassy surface, it may be that our genes carry an inborn preference for grassy landscapes. And what is carpet but an indoor Lawn, its texture yielding to the foot just like turf?

The problem here is that Lawn is not found in most parts of the world. For city dwellers, today's landscapes consist of expanses of concrete, asphalt, metal, glass, and plastic—no green in sight, except for the occasional tree or park. Surely, there's much in an urban setting for the eye to light upon, but it's man-made rather than natural, For most of the world, including city dwellers, Lawn is not a luxury or a status symbol; rather, it's an aberration. In places other than the U.S., the fronts of houses may abut the street, while inner courtyards are planted with trees and flowers; in other places, yards, bare of vegetation, consist of neatly swept earth; in yet other places, cottage gardens may surround dwellings, or vacant lots be turned into vegetable plots shared by a community. It seems that our supposedly genetic yen for Lawn is hardly universal.

So when I do away with my small expanse of green, I'm really reverting to the making of gardens, a practice that arose when we ceased to be hunter-gatherers and settled ourselves in villages. Yet, some Americans are positively addicted to Lawn. A friend, who serves as a Forest Service volunteer, greeting visitors who come to stay at a campground in the George Washington National Forest, tells me that campers often come to her pleading to be allowed to cut the grass. They've sold their houses and taken to the road in fifth wheels or land yachts, but, doggone, they miss their grass and all the hours spent to keep it up. So, in the vagabondage of retirement, these inveterate putterers toil away happily at something that once may have exasperated them and even driven them to bad language.

Lawn also turns some ordinarily law-abiding people into criminals. My cousin Patsy, who lives on Maryland's Eastern Shore, asks plaintively, "What do folks have against vines?" On either side of their lot, she and her family now have neighbors where once strawberries, watermelons, and soybeans grew. And the neighbors have put in lawns right up to the property lines. Patsy's side of the lines consisted of field edging—a natural mixture of mulberry and other trees, shrubs, honeysuckle, grapes and wisteria, poison ivy, orange daylilies, Queen Anne's lace, yarrow, and much else. Patsy describes what happened this way: "Somehow the new neighbors now want to control our side of the line. One neighbor felt compelled to cut down some of our well-established honeysuckle and grapevines. The other just sprayed Roundup on the wisteria and honeysuckle, killing the bridal veil and small trees as well. It seems to me if they had wanted some 'wilderness' to control, they should have planted ten less feet of lawn. I don't understand either their motivation to destroy the plants or their presumption to trespass. Maybe I need to reread Robert Frost and his words about good fences." The story does not end there. Patsy confronted the neighbor about his project to exterminate vines and other field edgings. But, he responded, he plans to naturalize the area by putting in azaleas and daffodils. "The suburban way," says Patsy. "Poison all the natural plants, then put in your own."

Obviously, Lawn induces madness. It's capable of destroying both good manners and good sense.

I exterminate the grass because Lawn is as sterile to my vision as a cityscape. Because it features only one color of the rainbow. Because it cramps the possibilities for biodiversity. Because it represents a war against nature and a brutally stubborn reassertion of the Christian West's assumption that God has granted dominion over everything else to humankind. My gardens, for all their color and life, make an ideological statement, for as I see it, my job—the human job—is to encourage nature's possibilities, to release its beauty, not to control it. And a garden is a place in which we can begin to understand our place in nature—that we are not apart from but rather inside of it.

The habitats that Lawn offers are few in number. On the other hand, my gardens and their trees not only furnish a haven for tomatoes but shelter an array of life from the minuscule to the middle-sized. Cardinals and catbirds perch on the tomato cages and nest, respectively, in the rose-of-Sharon bushes and the Norway spruce. Hummingbirds sip from the white and pink rose-of-Sharon blossoms. The birds attract the neighborhood's semiferal cats, but their hunting is not nearly so successful as that of the little male sharp-shinned hawk that perches on the chain-link fence and makes lightning-swift raids on the frequent gatherings of house sparrows. Bees haunt the blooming thyme. Swallowtail butterflies flit over the parsley in the raised bed and lay their eggs; the resulting caterpillars devour the parsley down to the ground, but the parsley forgives and grows lushly back. Cottontail rabbits of all sizes scamper amid the plants; to my astonishment, they have not dined on tender lettuce or newly sprouted beans—or, better said, not *yet*. Gray squirrels cavort in the trees and on the roof of the shed. They also play with immature eggplants, not eating these fruits the size of my thumb but just picking and scattering them hither and yon, all marked by sharp teeth. The eggplants could be caged, but it's easier to go to the local farmers' market when the urge for Parmigiana strikes. Both skunks and 'possums waddle regularly through the backyard. So do groundhogs, which have a bolt-hole under the shed. In the first year of the grass extermination project, I caught one of those critters sitting on its haunches smack-dab in the middle of the garden. Nor was it just sitting, no, it was chowing down on my cucumbers. Only five cukes in all were harvested. The groundhog never bothered anything else, not the lettuce, not the Hungarian wax peppers, and not the tomatoes. It was imperative, though, that I find a safe place for cukes. Where else but the front yard? There, groundhogs have no hidey-holes and are discouraged by the steady flow of human and canine traffic up and down the sidewalk. The first year's result: five plants of a pickling variety and forty-three fruits, enough for pot after pot of cuke-onion-vinegar salad.

With Lawn, you pretty well know what will happen next. With Garden, the surprises are endless.

TOOLS OF
THE TRADE

Once the relation between poetry
and the soil is well established
in the mind, all growing things
are endowed with more than
material beauty.

—*Elizabeth Lawrence*

R AKES, HOES, MATTOCK, SPADE, TROWEL, PRUNING
shears, maul, stakes, twine, baskets, five-gallon buckets—
gardening has always needed such tools. I store those with
long handles on the back porch in a rectangular plastic box three feet
high, while the short-handled sort are hung in brackets on a peg-
board affixed to the porch wall. The baskets and buckets, along with
the mini-tiller, rest on the floor below. In the first summer of my
full-time return to Tomato Haven, I went to a local builders' supply
store and bought a tall, five-shelf cabinet that now houses all manner of small items, including twine and scissors, sprinklers, a mark-
ing pen and little wooden markers, Miracle-Gro for the plants in
pots, and fertilizer stakes for the pear trees and junipers. Most of
these things can't be done without, except that cow or chicken manure could be substituted for chemical fertilizers. To my great good
fortune, a Carolina friend sent me home after a recent visit with a
bag so heavily laden with chicken droppings that I had go next door
to find help to lift it out of the trunk of my car.

Because most ordinary tools are of prehistoric provenance, they connect me with a long line of digging, sowing, reaping humanity. Granted, the earliest aids to gardening were sticks and stones, and twine was a strand of dried sinew or a willow withe. And what is my little tiller but a motorized harrow? Hands, of course, were the most important of all the farmer-gardener's tools. They still are. For hands hold the other tools, hands put seed in the earth, hands gather the harvest.

I go to some ancient accounts of the farmer's year. In his *Works and Days*, the Greek epic poet Hesiod, who composed in Homer's time or shortly thereafter, names maul and pruning hook. The poem as a whole is cautionary, advising piety lest the farmer call down divine wrath and have all his labor go for naught (never forget that the eye of Zeus sees everything). Nor should the farmer indulge in wintertime gossip over at the blacksmith's forge; no, indeed, he should stay home and busy himself around the house. He should also know the celestial signs that signal the time for planting, should know, too, which days are lucky and which are not. Nor should a man wade in a river without first washing his hands and so washing away his wickedness, as well. And, "A man should never wash his body in water a woman has used, for there is a dismal forfeit that comes in time also for this act." I read that and snort.

Then there is the Roman poet Virgil. In the last few years, I've divided my time between two worlds: the world that daily greets my senses—the one that rains or snows, the one that blooms and produces fruit, the one that daily purrs (two neutered tomcats, one black and white, the other a tiger, make their home with me)—and another world that's located on the farthest edge of the Christian millennia, the world of Italians working family farms in the first century B.C. The time machine that took me there was Virgil's *Georgics*, a four-book poem on farming. That's what the title means—it's the Greek word for "farming." And the four books deal respectively with crops and star signs that the farmer needs to know; with trees and grapevines; with livestock, especially cows and horses, sheep and goats; and, finally, with bees. For two years I lived inside its lines to make a translation using American—not British—English (it's the difference between "grain" and "corn," "boots" and "buskins," "sturdy twigs" and "truncheons"). Working through the Latin, I was joyfully surprised to discover the close connections between Then and Now. We see the same constellations. We use the same tools.

Who was Virgil? Who was this man who wrote a four-book love song to almost everything that grows or grazes on the land? With a few understandable exceptions, like snakes and grain-plundering mice, plants and animals alike receive his laud. But, like many lovers, he was also filled with doubts and blamed passion itself for much that may go awry. Despite the best human efforts, despite the most diligent, unremitting hard work, the world in which we live has never been made perfect. And Virgil's coming of age was filled with dispiriting, chaotic events—widespread political power grabs, corruption, civil wars, assassinations—which he was helpless to counter except in the singing of his poems. But he knew the land, knew it by heart.

Publius Vergilius Maro was born on October 15, 70 B.C., in Andes, a rural hamlet near Mantua in Cisalpine Gaul, now known as Lombardy. His parents, people of respectable means, came from peasant stock and were farmers. So, Virgil had been well acquainted from his earliest days with earth, farm animals, and crops. Educated at first in Cremona, Mantua, and Milan, he went south to the big city—Rome—at the age of seventeen. His studies, including Latin, Greek, and rhetoric, were precisely those that would appeal to any young man enamored of words and the music they make. He found a patron in a minister serving Octavian, later to become Augustus Caesar, and began to compose. His first poems were pastoral, dealing with shepherds; they were followed by the *Georgics*, published about 30 B.C. His masterwork, the *Aeneid*, appeared in 19 B.C., the year that he died.

One of the theses of the *Georgics* is that civilization and the existence of civil communities depend on agriculture. Virgil refers often in the poem to an age of Saturn, its overthrow by his son Jupiter, and the new era that ensued. The picture of Saturnian life is akin to that of the Big Rock Candy Mountains, with their cigarette trees and lemonade springs, all growing without human labor, all free for the taking. But when Jupiter vanquished the old order, it became necessary for humankind to work for a living. Fields required tilling, seeds and vines being set in the earth, animals training and pasturing—and they still do. From that time on we have no longer had access to innocent leisure. In one crucial sense, though it is a sense of which Virgil would have been unaware, the change from the golden age to one of labor was real. And it occurred when humanity learned to tame plants and animals. With that event, certain hitherto unthinkable phenomena transformed human existence. Because people were able to stay put, urban agglomerations became possible, along with the characteristics of city life, from noise to crowded slums. When the necessary cooperation found in tiny, tribal communities was lost, hierarchies developed with a rich and powerful few at the top and masses of serfs and slaves at the bottom. Wars became a way of life, either to protect everything already on hand or to gain more at the expense of others, be they neighbors or distant foes. In his nostalgia for a forever-lost golden age, Virgil shows an intuitive grasp of the havoc wrought in human life by urbanization and by warfare that appears to this day to be unending.

Many of the lines are possessed of great beauty. I feel that he speaks directly to me and my own labor when he writes lines like these, near the beginning of Book 4, in which he regrets not being able to include more fully in the poem some of the plants that have caught his fancy:

> Perhaps I should also sing what careful cultivation
> adorns rich gardens and the rose-beds of twice blooming Paestum,
> and how endives rejoice in the streams that they drink
> and the green banks, in their celery, and how the cucumber
> sprawling through the grass swells into a paunch. Nor should I be
> silent about the late-blooming narcissus or the flexible
> twigs of acanthus, pale ivy, and shore-loving myrtle.

As I read, imagination sees my own climbing red 'Blaze' roses, watches the cucumbers in the front yard produce their fine, fat, pickling-sized paunches, and picks the fragrant 'King Alfred' daffodils on the backyard terrace. Elizabeth Lawrence is right: there's an inescapable relationship between poetry and the soil.

There's also a relationship between poetry and the tools and techniques used to work the soil. Virgil mentions many tools, and they are the implements that we often use today—carts, hoes, rakes, and all the rest. His carts, open-ended wooden boxes with handles and a wheel, were forerunners of the modern wheelbarrow. And he's a true fanatic about wielding a hoe, which is needed to combat invaders:

> Unless you pursue the weeds with a relentless hoe,
> scare off the birds with shouting, remove the shade from over-
> shadowed farmland with a pruning hook, and call down rain with prayers,
> in vain, alas, you'll stare at someone else's heaps of grain
> and relieve your own hunger by shaking oak trees in the woods.

In other words, the diligent use of tools will keep you from having to live on acorns and other gleanings, catch as catch can.

Virgil would have been pleased by my two hoes, the favorites of all my tools, although their shapes are not those of his day, nor do I wield them as diligently as Virgil recommends. One is a homi, a forged steel hand-hoe of Korean provenance. I have two of them, one with a short handle, the other with a long. The short one was the tool used to uproot the grass as I sat on my three-legged stool in the front yard. Both of my homis have a business end with two sides, one straight and the other slightly rounded, that meet in a sharp point; this blade juts out at a right angle from the handle, and, oh, it slices with ease through grass, weeds, and dirt. It's also kind to my arthritic wrists. The other hoe at the top of my favorites list is a long-handled Circlehoe, which is also available in a short-handled version. Its name, patented like that of Kleenex and Sheetrock, describes the working end, which features a circular blade set at a slight angle to the handle. Only the part of the circle that touches earth is sharp. It allows the hoer to work close to plants' stems without disturbing the roots. Turn it over, pull it gently over the earth, and it smoothes the soil.

Virgil mentions a slew of commonsensical precepts that are as valid today as they were back then. When you grow vegetables, he advises that you:

- *Till the soil twice, once from end to end and once again across the newly made furrows.*
- *Rotate your crops.*
- *Water your plants, if the sky does not provide enough moisture.*

Crops were irrigated in his day. He describes the practice this way:

Need I mention him who, having sown the seed, tends the fields
hands on and vigorously levels piles of barren sand,
then diverts rivulets of running water to his crops
and, when the soil dries up, its sprouted grain burnt, in summer's heat—
behold!—brings water from the ridge through irrigation
channels? Falling, it rushes down the smooth stones with a hoarse
white noise and restores the thirsty soil with its bubbling jet.

But I live in town, where there are no rivulets to divert. It took decades for me to cotton on to the best ways to water plants. In the Carolina years, we used sprinklers—five-foot-high sprinklers that revolved and sent out jets of water and several kinds of low sprinklers that either rotated excitedly or oscillated gently back and forth. But there we drew our water from a well more than two hundred feet deep. Here in town, the city provides water and measures its usage. With this system, sprinklers are an expensive proposition. Mine whirled water over the plants and into the yard next door, no matter how carefully I tried to adjust the water pressure. But I flung water all over creation during the first summer of my full-time return to Tomato Haven, a summer characterized by the third year of a drought that baked and cracked the earth and turned the fields brown. Every other day, the oscillating-arm Green Thumb or the Rainswirl with its rotating head would be set in motion for half an hour amid the tomatoes. The crop was cornucopious; the water bill, sky-high. Luckily, rain fell abundantly the next summer, and the need for giving the tomatoes more to drink was almost nonexistent. Nonetheless, some watering is always needed to assure steady growth and production during the inevitable two- to three-week dry spells. Why did it take so long for me to discover an economical, far less wasteful means of watering? The answer is that, because sprinklers had always been part of my gardening efforts, I just couldn't see any further. Then, a daughter-in-law gave me a book called *The Garden That Cares for Itself*. Three years later, I began flipping through it for the first time, briefly scanning the color photographs. But the last section caught my attention: "Low-Care Vegetable Gardening." I started reading from beginning to end. And there it was—the secret that had eluded my fixation on sprinklers: the soaker hose. Herewith, a precept:

No sense in watering your neighbor's grass! A soaker hose made of porous rubber provides a cost-effective, water-conserving way to wet the whistle of any garden. Its open end attaches to a regular hose, while its closed end keeps the water contained. Place it beside the plants in your tomato or cole-crop patch, place it amid your flowers, then turn on the water, and the hose will deliver moisture directly where it's needed.

The soaker hose has also kept me from being drenched. In the past, I've sometimes been too lazy to turn off the water before moving the sprinkler; the result—an instant baptism with very cold water.

It's also possible to get a good sense of how much watering is needed. The precept goes as follows:

> *You can check on how much watering is needed by installing a rain gauge and checking with the county extension agent on average rainfall for your area. If the gauge shows enough rain has fallen to satisfy your plants, cut back on watering. Take up the gauge before frost, lest its contents freeze.*

Rainfall seems to satisfy plants far more than water from a tap.

Virgil's usefulness does not stop with good advice on irrigation. To my delight, I find that he gives perfectly valid instructions for two tests to see what kind of soil you're working with. The first involves considerable work, for it consists of digging a hole in the ground, filling it back up with the dirt extracted, and tamping it down with your feet. If the soil no longer fills the hole, it's loamy, but if you can't get all the soil back into the hole and some spills out, then the soil is compact and clayey. The second test is precisely that prescribed by the Rodale Press's *Garden Answers* book, published more than two thousand years after Virgil's death. You take the soil in your hand and squeeze. If it's loam, it crumbles when you knead it; it can't be molded into a ball. But a heavy, clayey soil will not only be compacted by a squeeze but will also retain the impression of the fingers. And, as Virgil sensibly says, "A heavy soil mutely makes itself known by its weight, so does a light one."

And Virgil teaches me something I should have known—the original nature of a grape arbor. His catalogue of wines from all over the Mediterranean makes me believe that he was a most appreciative oenophile, and his description of the grapes used in their making, so luscious that, were my yard a bit larger, I'd be tempted to put in some vines. Oh for "muscats from Rhodes, fit for gods' palates and those of men" and "native grapes with clusters big as breasts"! He gives detailed instructions on setting in the vines and training them to climb their arbors. Before living within the *Georgics*, I'd made the casual assumption that an arbor was an archway, a trellis, or the wires strung between wooden posts that you see in a modern vineyard. A Roman arbor was none of these. It was just that—an *arbor*, which is the Latin word for "tree." The grapevines were trained to wind their way up oaks and elms.

In addition to the tools and techniques familiar to both Italian farmers and modern gardeners, not to mention the generations in between, I use other garden devices not mentioned in the *Georgics* but certainly known to farmers in Virgil's day—compost bins, a raised bed, and a cold frame.

COMPOST

Compost piles have existed since people began to raise crops and animals. They are not simply a convenient place to toss the trash. Dung, urine, green manure in the form of plant and food scraps, decaying leaves, wood shavings, ashes—all of these and more have been consigned for millennia to pits, heaps, and bins, a practice that leads to a precept:

What you take from the earth may be returned to increase its fertility.

People who practiced this kind of recycling did not, until recently, think of it in those terms; they simply noticed that plants treated with compost grew better than those that weren't. The virtues of dung and urine are that the former abounds in phosphates, while the latter is rich in nitrogen and potash. These three ingredients are found in various ratios in the commercial fertilizers available today at garden centers, hardware stores, and farm coops.

I remember a radio show (the name of which eludes me) that was presented on NPR sometime in the 1990s. It dealt with garden triumphs and gave out first-, second-, and third-place awards to gardeners who had succeeded in a truly original fashion. The top prize was once received by a woman whose shrubbery, planted beside the house, had thrived beyond her fondest hope. The secret was that it had been well fertilized by her husband, who'd pissed upon it daily during the spring.

I also remember the system that was used from the early 1900s until the early 1950s to transport the droppings and urine of the Jerseys and Guernseys in the cow barn at my father's Ohio farm. At milking time and in cold weather, the animals, their necks fastened in stanchions, were housed on a raised concrete platform covered with straw. Behind the platform, right under the cows' tails, lay a trough that received their solid and liquid ordure. A railing overhead was bedecked by small buckets that could be lowered to scoop up the contents of the trough, raised again by a pulley, and moved out through the open barn door to be dumped in a rectangular manure pit, built of brick, that must have been at least six by twelve feet in size. The cows' bedding straw was added to the pit manually. After decomposition had occurred, a section of well rotted straw and manure would be removed and tilled into the large truck garden. I know for a fact, however, that the manure pit held more than straw and dung, for once, in my teenaged years, a tomato sprawled and bore fruit in its northeast corner.

My own compost bin is a yard-high square box made of sturdy black plastic with a tight-fitting lid that's perforated to let in rainwater. Compost likes to be somewhat damp in order to cook scraps into soil. And the bin eats many kinds of scraps, from potato and banana peels, melon rinds, and onion skins to dried leaves, dryer lint, and newspapers. The only forbidden items are meats and fats, which become over-fragrant when they rot. A foot-high door sits at the bottom of the bin's front; lift it and behold the miracle—dark, friable dirt.

But some things should never go into a composter of any sort. Needless to say, plastics and metal are not welcome, nor are large branches (though sawdust would definitely do). The main organic materials to avoid are weeds, especially those that have gone to seed, for seeds don't invariably disintegrate but remain viable for an unconscionably long time. (You've heard, perhaps, the true tales of seeds discovered in ancient tombs that have sprouted when planted several thousand years later.) In fact, just about any seeds that land in compost will germinate. The patch on the south side of the front yard, duly dressed with compost that was tilled in, brought forth cantaloupe and tomato sprouts. I ruthlessly pulled up the former— too much competition for the cucumbers—but allowed the latter to remain. They did not bear fruit but did look decorative with their fernlike leaves, a needed touch of cheerful green after the daylilies surrounding the cukes had been cut back after they'd bloomed. But what to do with weeds? Country places have their on-site dumps, but here's a precept for a garden in the heart of town:

Acquire an inexpensive wheeled trash can with a lid. Stash your weeds within, and when it's full, roll it out to the curb for collection. This method avoids clogging landfills with weed-stuffed polyethylene bags that last forever and keep their contents intact. But unbagged weeds will vanish in a landfill, which is, after all, a gigantic compost heap.

I've used several types of compost bins, including a batch com-poster—a monstrous black plastic thing, the size of a barrel, that's spun around daily to mix the contents. It's supposed to make compost in only three weeks. But its digestion is finicky, and it cannot handle tough old tomato vines and sticks of any size, which emerge in very much the same sassy condition as when they went in. Once, in my Carolina days, I had a bin that needed stirring; to decompose properly, the contents had to be churned with a pitchfork—hard work! Some people prefer yard-square compost boxes built of wire or boards, but this type also needs stirring. A friend who is a Total Gardener just heaps up clippings, leaves, and weeds in unobtrusive places. I'm happy, though with my present bin—square, well-ventilated, and ideal for those (like me) who are elderly and/or lazy. Put scraps in at the top, take good dirt out at the bottom. A trowel or spade is all you need to remove the finished compost. This most satisfactory compost bin required two years for the transformation of starter materials to usable compost (for a larger household with more scraps, less time would do), but my wait was worthwhile. The very first haul consisted of ten gallons of healthy soil to put in the front yard's cucumber and cole patch. Later that year, several more gallons were ready, and they had begun to be enriched by worm castings, which are nothing other than worm manure—the stuff that has passed through their digestive systems and been excreted.

⤳ WORMS

The worms in the compost bin came there by accident. They are red wigglers (*Eisenia fetida*), slender but feisty dark red creatures that dwell above the soil in damp leaf litter and other moist places. (Such litter- and compost-loving worms are epigeic worms, while anecic worms, like nightcrawlers (*Lumbricus terrestris*), live within the soil, and endogeic worms are those found in the roots of plants.) Red wigglers weren't supposed to be in the compost bin, no indeed. Their intended home was a worm bin—the Worm Factory—com-posed of four black trays and a lid, eighteen inches square and twenty-four inches high, with a valve to remove the liquid that accumulates in the bottom tray. The bin sits unobtrusively in my dining room. The dining room, cleared only twice a year for Thanksgiving and Christmas, is more properly my nest, in which I am surrounded by five well-filled bookcases, file boxes, an easy chair, a sideboard containing rubber bands and floppy disks, a wooden bookcase that holds CDs, and a computer desk. The dining table is also a desk, the surface of which is covered by dictionaries, envelopes, and drifts of paper. And my nest is the place in which two pounds of red wigglers were ensconced when they arrived in May. Listless at first, they regained their wiggle after two days and began chowing down on every kitchen scrap that I could provide. Like compost bins, worms are not happy with meat and fat, but vegetables, lint, and newspapers soon disappear. Friends began saving their banana peels, eggshells, and breadcrusts, which would arrive in gallon plastic milk jugs with the narrow tops cut off. One houseguest sent a very large envelope that included not only a thank-you note but also much shredded newspaper.

Why worms? Two separate encounters made them seem creatures that I could not do without. The first happened at the local farmers' market, where one of the vendors sold worm castings by the pint, quart, gallon, and twenty-pound bag. They were expensive, but the south side of the front yard urgently needed nutrients added to its nearly sterile red clay soil. I toted home a twenty-pound sack and also heeded the vendor's suggestion that garden lime be added as well to the soil. Castings and lime were applied, then tilled in, along with some nitrogen-supplying alfalfa meal. (The farm coop sells alfalfa meal only in fifty-pound bags; so, there was much left over after my spring crop of onions had been dressed.) The following year, I'd learned that worm manure could be generated and harvested right in my own house. My absentee instructor was garden-columnist Amy Stewart, whose book *The Earth Moved: On the Remarkable Achievements of Earthworms* convinced me by page 24 that keeping red wigglers was an eco-friendly act, and, just imagine, no more shelling out big bucks to the castings man. As it happened, however, the castings man did not return for the new season at the farmers' market. No matter: I could do it myself.

Or so I thought. Goodness knows, the bin was crawling with worms—little worms, big worms, and worms in between. The bin's interior was as it should be—moist but not sopping. The finest food was supplied daily, along with fresh bedding. After a month and a half, I gathered a quart of castings. Not long after that, the red wigglers started slipping out of the bin's cracks onto the floor. Something in wormville was not right. It was as if its inhabitants were trying desperately to escape. Each morning, I'd find dessicated carcasses, like little dark-red threads, embellishing not only the floor and Persian rugs in my nest but the gray kitchen carpet as well. Each afternoon, I'd find fewer and fewer live residents in the Worm Factory. Then, there seemed to be none at all. I cleaned the trays, putting bedding and uneaten food into the outdoor compost bin—no sense in wasting things that could be recycled.

Understanding the problems took time. To begin with, the instructions that came with the Worm Factory are lethally inaccurate. The manual says, for example, that the liquid that drains to the bin's lowest tray is "commonly known as Worm Tea," which "is a great liquid fertilizer for your houseplants or garden. We recommend you mix it with equal parts of water first." But the liquid, which had to be drained off every day, had a foul odor. Just what is worm tea, anyway? I found a knowledgeable vermiculturist at North Carolina State University, who gave me the facts. Worm tea, formally known as castings tea, is made from worm castings that are steeped in a utensil manufactured specially for this purpose—a compost tea brewer; the tea makes a fine fertilizer. But the excess liquid in the bottom tray is the antithesis of worm tea. The expert tells me that it is a leachate, which "collects in the bottom of the bin after it has passed through undigested material (i.e., whatever is being fed to the worms, such as animal manure or food waste). Undigested material is dangerous because it could contain human pathogens and plant toxins. You should not pour this liquid on plants." The leachate, however, was not affecting the worms adversely. The difficulties, not one but two, lay elsewhere.

Obedient to the instructions in the manual, I was not only over-feeding the worms but also giving them toxic material. A teachers' guide issued by the Texas Natural Resource Conservation Commission set me straight. How much food do worms need? Worms actually eat the bacteria that break down the materials put into their bin, but it's up to the wormkeeper to give the bacteria something to work on. The owner's manual says, "The general rule of thumb is to feed one pound of worms one half pound of food per day," while the teachers' guide says, "Start with a pound of worms for each pound of food scraps you intend to compost each week." So, the manual calls for three and a half times as much food as *Eisenia fetida* really needs. No wonder the bin became whiffy. I find the same disagreement when it comes to paper bedding, which the worms also consume. Here's the word from the manual: "Shredded paper—especially the glossy inserts, is coated with clay which the worms love." So, I regularly shredded the inserts, moistened them, and put them into the bin (it's truly helpful to have a crosscut paper shredder). The guide, however, issues a caution: "Some colored inks contain traces of toxic materials." The moral is, use regular newsprint, not the pages with colored ink.

It was sorrowful to think that I'd killed my worms. Except that I hadn't. But that fact was not immediately apparent. A month later, I opened the door of the compost bin. Oh my! There'd been a resurrection! A few worms wriggled actively through a mixture of castings and finished compost. By early fall, the colony had become dense. It looked as if there were more red wigglers than compost.

Red wigglers, along with many other genera, are members of the class Oligochaeta, a Greek word meaning "few bristles." (Oligochaetologist is the name for someone who studies earthworms.) On first consideration, it may seem odd that worms have bristles, but bristles figure in their sex lives, a matter that I'll get to shortly. And worms belong to the Lubricidae family, which takes its name from *lubricus*, the Latin word for "earthworm." Once upon a time, in the days of the Roman naturalist Pliny (A.D. 23–79), *lubricus* was a word of abuse when hurled at someone else: "You *worm!*"

As for their sex lives, the reproductive habits of red wigglers and many of their kin are passing strange. They are hermaphrodites, and mating, an act that can take hours, involves matching the male sexual organs—the pores—of one partner to the female pores of the other, and vice versa. To keep from slithering away from each other, they hang on by using their setae, which are little bristles near their pores, and they also excrete a sticky fluid that keeps them glued together. The fluid forms a partial tube around each body. When it hardens, the worm slides out of this tube leaving behind egg and sperm, which have not yet joined. When the worm makes its exit, the ends of the tube come together to form a cocoon. Then, fertilization can take place, although such may not occur for weeks or months, depending on external conditions—temperature and moisture. When the cocoons hatch, the young are fully worm in nature, miniature versions of their parents. The miracle in my compost bin came about because the material that was added when I cleaned out the worm habitat contained cocoons that my inexperienced eye had been unable to spot.

Red wigglers help a garden in many ways, notably in adding calcium to the soil. And calcium helps plants take up nitrogen, which triggers leaf growth. Amy Stewart, who conned me into worm farming, says this of red wigglers: "They address calcium deficiencies on several fronts, producing calcium in their calciferous glands during digestion, adding it to the soil through their castings, or even transforming it, as it moves through the intestine, into a form that is easier for plants to absorb."

Red wigglers are happiest at moderate temperatures from 40° to 80°. But it's cold here in the winter, and the temperature can dip as low as 5° above zero. The habitat waits in my nest. The order for a pound of worms has already been placed.

❧ RAISED BEDS

Raised beds are nothing unusual in the annals of gardening. A garden historian writes, "The earliest references to the raised-bed system are

Roman, but the technique was doubtless practiced by civilizations older than theirs; it was also adopted by the Moors of southern Spain and the earliest monastic gardeners." Often, irrigation channels separated the beds. Carrots insisted that I construct a raised bed, and I filled it with bags of nearly black commercial garden soil.

The desire to build such a bed was triggered by the unexpected arrival of carrot seeds. Two packets of the 'Sweet Sunshine' variety came as "free gifts," accompanying an order that I'd placed with the Burpee Company. ("Free gifts"—hmpf, a common but obnoxiously redundant expression.) Carrots, however, do not achieve their typically long, straight form in stony soil like that in my yard. Because they can't move the stones, they twist and kink around the little chunks of limestone that get in their way. A carrot grown in such soil may look like a spiral or a corkscrew. I had a choice: forego carrots or make a raised bed. Herewith, a precept:

A raised bed may be built in one of several ways. Railroad ties may be arranged or boards nailed together in any shape that you wish. Corners may be purchased from garden supply houses and boards at the local lumberyard. Or, soil may simply be heaped up and a drainage ditch dug around the perimeter. Fill it with soil from your yard, commercial garden soil, or the leaf-and-chipped-wood compost that many municipalities give away for the asking.

I followed the path of buying metal corners into which boards were inserted. The result: a sturdy six-by-four foot bed that is ten inches deep. The garden soil that fills it is marvelously friable. A friend commented that it was the biggest cat litter box she'd ever seen, but, for reasons known only to themselves, the neighborhood's semiferal cats (many of which wear collars) have not used it. The animals that find it to their liking are the gray squirrels, which have stashed black walnuts in the depths of the soil. They sprout, and I pluck. The carrots have been happy—nor are they alone but grow amid other annuals like basil, marigolds, and zinnias.

Does a raised bed have virtues other than allowing carrots to grow straight down?

> *Raised beds offer deep-rooted plants ample growing room. They also provide better drainage, especially in regions of high rainfall, where good drainage makes the difference between a plant's drowning or thriving.*

A second raised bed has now joined the first—a circular bed with three tiers to which a hose may be attached to water plants with a gentle spray. It might hold any number of annuals, but I'll set in strawberries bought at the farmers' market. Visions of jam jars dance in my head.

COLD FRAMES

A cold frame is a gardening device that Virgil would have known about. Pliny tells of a rolling vegetable patch built to satisfy the cucumber cravings of the emperor Tiberius (42 B.C.–A.D. 37). The cucumbers were planted in beds with wheels so that his gardeners could roll them easily into the sunshine; on chilly days, the beds were covered with glazed frames. The British botanist John Gerard's 1633 *Herball* tells of another kind of bed for growing cukes: a "bed of hot and new horse dung taken forth of the stable (and not from the dunghill)." But this is a hotbed, in this case heated by the decay of manure, which may still be used for this purpose. One current method of creating a hotbed calls for digging a pit, shoveling in eighteen inches of horse manure mixed with straw, and covering it with six inches of good soil. Another kind of hotbed was warmed by buried pipes carrying hot water. Nowadays, seedlings may be started and kept cozy by thermostat-controlled electric propagating mats laid on the bed or by plug-in electric cables laid out in soil or sand beneath the starter pots.

A cold frame, however, relies on other sources of heat. It traps sunlight during the day and gathers heat radiated from the soil at night. And it's a convenient, space-saving way to start seeds outdoors before weather and soil-temperatures allow them to be sown directly in the ground. In my Carolina days, April brought temperatures warm enough to set the starter pots with seeds out on a deck, nor did they need to be covered at night. But Staunton, with its 1400-foot elevation and its more northerly location, makes this casual kind of starting impossible. I did have choices, though. One was to wait until air and earth warmed up; the second, to purchase vegetable and flower seedlings at the farmers' markets; and the third, to set up a cold frame. It took three years for a working cold frame to become reality.

I remember the cold frames on my father's farm—long, low rectangular boxes with sides that sloped downward from back to front and lids made of old windows. Holding a deep bed of earth (surely well enriched by cow manure), they were set on the south side of a barn where they'd get the most springtime sun. There, the tomatoes, melons, squash, cukes, bell peppers, and beets were started. On really warm days, the window lids were propped open early so that the tender sprouts wouldn't cook; in the late afternoon, the lids were closed to keep in the day's heat. How they were watered, I don't know, but moisture was likely delivered regularly by a hose. I also remember the lushness of the truck garden when the seedlings were transplanted— the curling tendrils on the vines, the yellow tomato blossoms, the red-veined green leaves of the beets.

Clearly, Tomato Haven needed a cold frame. I found two different building plans. One calls for beginning the frame by finding an old wooden storm window, the size of which determines the frame's dimensions. The back, front, and sides are made of 2x8-inch cedar planks, cut to match the size of the window. Then the boards are glued together, three high for the back and sides, two for the front, and made secure with screws. Last of all, the window lid is then attached to the back with hinges. The building plan calls for keeping a stick handy to prop up the lid on hot days. The second plan uses plywood, with pieces cut so that the sides interlock. The top consists of clear, heavy plastic stapled in place. To ventilate this model, you simply grab the bottom of the front panel, lift it up, and put a prop under it. Easy enough, the two of them—if you have the tools and the inclination. I lacked both.

Catalogues beckoned, along with the Internet. I found several kinds of cold frame that looked as if they'd work well, and I ordered one described as "Dutch." High in the back, low in the front, it was a box made of insulated polycarbonate panels that were put together by being slid into profiles—corners, that is—made of heavy-duty green plastic. The lid consisted of another cut-to-fit sheet of polycarbonate. When the profiles were attached, the panels would hook together and form the cold frame. The box had no bottom panel; it rested right on the ground. The front yard offered the perfect place for it—a south-facing spot near the rosemary and sage. The package arrived in good time. I opened it, spread out the pieces in an orderly fashion, and set to work. The instructions said that assembly would take only twenty minutes. It took four hours. I should have been warned when the package arrived that its contents were something other than those described on the Web site. To begin with, the outside of the package stated that it was *Deutsch*—German—not Dutch. Then, the corners were all longer than the panels they were supposed to fit, but I didn't know that until I'd spread the panel edges with vegetable oil so that they'd slide more easily into the profiles. I got out my coping saw and cut those corners to fit the panels. Everything should have been returned to the dealer posthaste, but the time to start seeds had come, and, doggone, that's what was going to happen. Late on the afternoon of the cold frame's arrival, it was set out in the front yard. On the very next day, which was April 26, the birthday of John James Audubon, I fetched starter pots from the shed. These pots deserve a precept:

> *Save the small four- or six-cell starter pots that held the tomato and other seedlings that you bought at a farmers' market or garden center. They'll come in handy when you start your own seeds at home.*

The seeds were sown and watered, and the pots were set out in the brand-new cold frame. I made a journal entry recording what was planted—basil, parsley, catnip, cayenne peppers, bleeding heart, zinnias, and sunflowers. All that was needed was to open the lid on warm days, close it against the chill of spring nights, and apply water daily.

Except that, after the seeds had sprouted and begun to put out secondary leaves, another problem sprang into being. It was as if I'd sown dragon's teeth and silent enemies had risen from the soil. Something was nibbling and gnawing the tender leaves.

It didn't take long to catch the enemies at work—slugs and snails that were sneaking under the bottom of the cold frame where it did not lie flat on the ground. The remedy, not entirely effective, was to sprinkle the earth below the starter pots with diatomaceous earth. The earth, comprising mainly silicon dioxide, sticks to the soft snail and slug bodies; because it cannot be removed, they die. I'd really fix those mollusks once and for all the following spring by placing screening underneath the frame. But as it happened, I made the mistake of leaving the cold frame in the yard, where a twelve-inch snowfall caused it to collapse. All the king's horses and all the king's men couldn't put cold frame together again.

In January, when the gardening catalogues arrive in a spate, I spied another cold frame that looked sturdier. It did not rest directly on the ground but was elevated to waist-height by an aluminum stand. Not only did the stand support the box but it also possessed a shelf of its own. Like the "Dutch" cold frame, it was made of insulated polycarbonate panels. Unlike that most unsatisfactory box, it advertised a bolt-together assembly. I got out a magnifying glass and peered at the small color photo in the catalogue: it did indeed have bolts. It also came with a floor of green plastic panels for the box. But it was three times more expensive than the model that collapsed under the weight of snow. For two months, I pondered making such an investment but came up with a precept:

Invest in the best, for cheaper is not always better. This principle is as true of cold frames as it is of trowels and other tools. Cheap trowels will bend at the juncture of handle and blade when used to lift earth out of the ground. Cheap cold frames can't be reassembled if they fall apart.

I picked up the phone and ordered the cold frame. It took only three days to arrive from Washington State, clear across the country. And it was so easy to assemble that I did not find one single moment of frustration. On April 23, the starter pots were sown with the seeds of 'Little Leaf' cucumbers, 'Joe's Long Cayenne' peppers, hot jalapeños with the varietal name of 'Conchos', and rust-red sunflowers. The peppers took forever to sprout, but sprout and bear they finally did. The cukes, however, came up exactly one week after they'd been tucked into the potting soil.

A precept governs the watering of starter pots:

Both in a cold frame and in the open air, the watering of newly started seeds is made easier by the use of capillary mats.

The use of capillary watering techniques, which give plants a small, steady supply of moisture, is nothing new. I've found a drawing of a method used in the 1300s—a water-filled pot that is suspended from a branch and delivers water, drop by drop, from a feather placed in a small hole in the bottom of the pot. The dealer who purveys the elevated cold frame also carries a capillary system—a 22x16-inch plastic tray with a cover over which a thirsty capillary mat is stretched. The tray acts as a reservoir, and the mat, constantly dewy as it sops up the water, provides a steady supply of moisture to the pots. In spring my two trays reside in the cold frame. But come July, when it's time to start seedlings for the fall crops of cauliflower and broccoli, the trays are set out on a table on the front porch, for summer heat turns the interior of a cold frame into an oven. In fall, the cold frame is stashed on the front porch until spring (thank goodness for Tomato Haven's capacious front porch).

Virgil speaks of tools as "militant farmers' weapons." And weapons they are, fighting weeds, keeping entropy at bay. Our battles are just, for they support the causes of sprouting, bloom, and fruition, of human need and human delight. Gardens past, gardens present, and gardens to come—the tools we use connect each one to every other. So do getting our hands dirty with soil, our fingernails black with basil juice, our noses sunburned. We're part of a tradition fourteen millennia old.

HOW A
GARDEN GROWS

Gardening,
reading about gardening,
writing about gardening
are all one;
no one gardens alone.

—*Elizabeth Lawrence,*
The Little Bulbs

G ARDENS GROW IN MANY WAYS. I GARDEN IN CON-
sortium with friends, fellow gardeners, seed catalogues and
nurseries, hungry birds, nut-burying squirrels, and Lady
Luck. Seeds sprout—behold, basil, hot peppers, sunflowers. Nurseries present irresistible temptations—thread-leaved coreopsis
(*Coreopsis verticillata*), hens and chicks, (*Sempervivum soboliferum*),
a Seckel pear tree (*Pyrus communis*). Then, people give plants from
their own gardens—the daylilies (*Hemerocallis* species) that have
run riot and the blue and cerise spiderworts (*Tradescantia virginiana*). My Illinois daughter-in-law contributed a cutting from her
corkscrew willow (*Salix matsudana tortuosa,* "contorted willow from
Matsuda," in the Orient), which I rooted and planted; now the tree,
with its kinked branches, is twice as tall as I. Not long ago, the market master of the local farmers' market gave my garden a candy lily
(*Pardacanda x norrisii*), which isn't a lily at all but rather a cross between the blackberry lily and the vesper iris, all three of them members of the Iris family. The volunteers are not to be overlooked,

either—annuals like cosmos (*Cosmos bipinnatus*) that sow themselves, rose-of-Sharon bushes (*Hibiscus syriacus*) popping up everywhere, and trees, a boggling number of trees, that come from who
knows where. My garden grows by outright theft, as well—I'll tell
about that in a moment. And chance plays a part, as it did in the case
of the pompom bushes.

The basement apartment in which I lived at the end of the 1970s
and in the early 1980s—the apartment that faced my thief-ridden
tomato patch—was reached by a set of limestone steps that led from
the sidewalk down to my front (and only) door. The dirt on either
side of those steps was thick with weeds. Dandelions, briars, Spanish
needle, a mort of others—nature was at work again: if there is vacant
space, it shall be occupied. That holds true for all living things, and
the fastest off the mark, the most opportunistic, is the one that wins
territory. If ground is cleared, it won't stay bare for long. I cannot
guess what chosen flowers or shrubs may have grown in the past beside the steps or how they might have been cleared away. Most likely,
they succumbed to neglect, and the weeds jumped in gleefully. After
contemplating those undesirables for a year or so, I had no choice
but to put paid to their insouciance and install something less tough
but more lovely. Clearing away the weeds began as soon as the
thought was consciously formed.

What next? The yard did not belong to me. I was willing to invest my time and energy in putting gardens on either side of the
steps, but my purse was lean. Enter chance. On springtime birding
expeditions in the Blue Ridge Mountains, a friend and I had noticed that in widely scattered places the woods contained small
pockets of garden-bright color. Things like tulips, daffodils, and
flowering shrubs were abloom amid the trees. They didn't get there
by themselves—no, someone had planted them. They marked old
homesteads. Sometimes we'd see tumbledown boards; more often,
only the rubble of a stone chimney would indicate the site of a
cabin. We took to traveling with a shovel, a trowel, and baskets into
which to put our trophies. From one expedition, I brought home

kerria and planted it along the east side of the steps, where it would make a green shield against the cinder-block walls of the next-door neighbor's Him Room, a space under the back porch that had been newly enclosed and reserved for the sole, bibulous use of the man of the house.

Kerria japonica—a wonderful shrub, sometimes called Japanese rose or Japanese globeflower. The only member of its genus, it belongs to Rosaceae, the Rose family. And the genus-name comes from William Kerr, a Scot who tended Kew Gardens in London and also collected plants in China, Java, and the Philippines. In his day, plant collection was a great excuse for international adventure, and many botanists and botanizers took to far-flung travel. Kerria's species-name—"of Japan"—is a misnomer, for the plant is in fact native to southwestern China; the mistake seems to have occurred because the first description that reached Europe was made of a plant found in Japan. Kerr sent a double-flowered specimen home from China in 1804. It comes in single-flowered cultivars, as well. Whatever the cultivar, it sends out slender, trailing branches as graceful as a willow's and in spring bursts into profuse bloom. The one that I brought home is known as 'Pleniflora', "lots of flowers," which covers itself with masses of small, double yellow blossoms as round as pompoms. What a gift from a long-gone stranger who had settled in the mountains!

Several pompom bushes installed, the Him Room's dull gray cinder blocks concealed, I still needed greenery for the eighteen-inch-wide strip of earth on the west side of the steps. At that point, serendipity assumed human form. It may have been that word of my desire had gone out among the ladies of the local garden club, of which my mother was a member. It may have been that I'd made mention of my naked earth during conversations at the grocery store. Whatever the cause, the phone began to ring. And the generosity of gardeners knew no bounds: they offered enough plants to cover ten strips the size of mine. Calla lilies, daylilies, Asiatic lilies, irises, bee balm, artemesia, and more—the choices seemed infinite. But it was necessary to be somewhat selective, for my strip lay in shadow for much of the day, and its soil was poor. The selection was finally made from the gardens of the doyenne of daffodils, my mother's friend who had not only served as president of the American Daffodil Society but was an expert judge of that golden—and pink and white and orange—host. The gardens surrounding her house, however, comprised far more than daffodils. On her advice, I settled on anemones (*Anemone x hybrida*) and astilbe (*Astilbe x arendsii*), both of them perennial. She dug them up with great vigor, placed them in the baskets that I'd brought for the occasion, and instructed me to give her a call if I needed more.

I said, "Oh, this is lovely. Th—"

Sternly, she interrupted. "Don't say it. Never thank anyone who gives you plants. It blights them."

"Then I won't say it. I'll just go home and dig holes."

"Give them a big drink when you put them in. They'll appreci-ate that. Now, be off with you."

And off I went, toting with me not only my new treasures but also a slow-burning curiosity about the origin of such a superstition. A full quarter of a century passed before I began to investigate. The quest for answers started with asking friends who garden if they knew of this peculiar custom. More did than didn't. Elsie had heard of it when she lived in Illinois, and Tess had picked it up in Indiana. Jeffery Beam, a friend who is a poet, a passionate gardener, and also the assistant to the botanical librarian at a renowned university, al-lowed as how he'd heard it when he was growing up in a part of Pennsylvania that had been settled by Germans. He also sent me a copy of an article, written more than a hundred years ago, on the folklore found in German areas of North Carolina. One tidbit states, "Never thank anyone who gives you seed; if you do, they will never do any good."

Seed? That figures, for it's part and parcel of a plant. And the fact that this notion has connections with Germany means that the Old World—most likely not just Germany but all of Europe and (I wouldn't be surprised) Africa and Asia as well—have the habit of

Not-Thanking for certain items, be they whole plants or seeds or something else entirely. In Italy, for example, Not-Thanking is de rigueur if someone gives you fire for a cigarette or a blaze on the hearth. I sense reverse magic at work here: it is not appropriate to thank anyone for something that was stolen in the first place, and stolen from the gods themselves. How presumptuous—no, how perilous—to render thanks for something humankind is not supposed to have! Nor are you supposed to thank fairies for providing favors. To thank them means that their services are no longer required, and at being so spurned, they may fly into a terrible rage (as happens with house-elves in the Harry Potter stories).

The hundred-year-old article given to me by Jeffery points me in the direction of consulting a present-day specialist in folklore. Karen Baldwin, who teaches the subject at East Carolina University, has been a friend for years. I first met her when she attended a talk about birds that I gave at the North Carolina Maritime Museum. Not much later, she and her husband, avid birders both, came along on one of the birding and botanizing field trips that the museum regularly led through my territory on the banks of North Carolina's wide and salty river Neuse. One thing led to another: we began corresponding and visiting. I've also sat in on Karen's classes. But only in the late spring of 2004, when Karen and her husband come to my Virginia house for supper (not only have they come but they have also brought salmon and pilaf), does it occur to me to ask her if she can provide an answer to the question, Why are thanks unwelcome?

"There's an analogy," she says. "A traditional healer is not to be thanked. Thanks vitiate the cure, annihilate its power. Not thanking is widespread in the South, and it doesn't matter who you are— black, white, Houma Indian (that's a tribe in Louisiana). Healing is not something done *by* me but *through* me. And you know that the relationship between the healer and the kitchen gardener is very close. The simples, the material medica, come from the garden."

"So if I thank, then I annihilate the power of the gift? The plant will shrivel and die?"

"That's it," Karen replies and digs back into the salmon.

To garden, then, is to be engaged in something healing, something magical.

You want to know, of course, about theft. It's not like helping myself to the pompom bushes, for those were ownerless and abandoned. If there are degrees of thievery, this one may be more serious than that perpetrated by the squirrels and landlady who stole my tomatoes. I prefer, however, to think of my recent activities not as stealing but as taking something that is derelict, like apples fallen from a tree. It's also liberation—plant liberation, the equivalent of springing an innocent being from prison. For doesn't a smothering of weeds imprison a flower?

The place in which liberation occurred was the yard of the brick house on the uphill side of mine. I've known that yard far longer than have its present owners. When I moved to Tomato Haven, the house was occupied by the elderly couple who had built it in the 1930s. She gave me a blue garter, a practice piece for the one she'd make for a granddaughter, to wear at my wedding to the Chief. On that occasion, I did not indulge in Not-Thanking, no indeed. Her husband was yard-proud. Always formally dressed in hat, jacket, and tie, he'd putter for hours outside to keep the grass neat and the weeds out of the flower beds. And, oh, there were flowers—irises and Asiatic lilies in front, wistaria shading the front porch, multihued four o'clocks along the foundation on the south side of the house, lilies of the valley in a shady spot in the backyard, two forsythia bushes with trunks as big around as my forearm, and, right next to my yard, tiny old-fashioned irises with gold standards and rust-colored falls. But he died in the early '90s. With regular yard help from a son-in-law, she continued to live in the house until she became so frail that a daughter took her in. That's when the weeds started taking over. By the time the new owners moved in, the yard had pretty well been subsumed by a tanglement of undesirables. Goldenrod reared up amid the lilies of the valley. Wild clematis with its frothy white flowers cloaked the forsythia, while morning glory vines wound themselves around every branch. Then a plant with leaves looking for all the world like those of zucchini or butternut squash sprawled across the grass and climbed up a side of the screened-in back porch, shading it completely. I waited for golden squash blossoms. Nothing happened except that the greenery extended itself daily. It grew as rapaciously as kudzu. Finally, however, it put out flowers—tiny white flowers that grew from the sides of slender six-inch spikes. I took pictures, scanned the photos, and sent them off to my friend Jeffery. A reply arrived on the very same day: bur cucumber, *Sicyos angulatus* "angled cucumber," a widespread native weed. I learned not long after why "bur" is part of its common name: the tiny yellow fruits are covered with sharp spines. I called the neighbors to let them know the plant's identity. Eventually, it was removed, but not before its seeds had broadcast themselves about into adjoining yards. (The neighbors are Luddites, who do not believe in power tools. A muscle-driven push mower trims the grass and weeds.) The next year, bur cucumber had begun to climb my towering Norway spruce. So I just walked through the Luddites' yard and uprooted it, along with a sprawling host of others.

The old-fashioned irises, however, were not victims of bur cucumber vines but rather of a whole gang of muggers—ground ivy, Indian strawberry, red clover, morning glories. They had not only covered the irises but twisted themselves into a strangling knot. It's a good thing that the market master had given me the candy lily, for as I was planting it next to the stone wall that divides my yard from that of the Luddites, I spotted the little flowers glowing gold in the weed-shadow. It took only ten minutes to fill the watering can, make holes in the ground near the candy lily, dig up a bunch of irises, transplant them, and tamp the earth down firmly around their watered rhizomes. When they'll bloom again is impossible to predict, for irises can dilly-dally, sometimes taking years to send up flower stalks after they've been subjected to the indignities of upheaval. But, giving good reason for hope, the leaves of the newly set-in irises are perky, not limp. I look upon them without a shred of guilt. The feeling is rather one of happiness that living plants have been rescued from the brink of doom. The lilies of the valley are next on the liberation list. Amid their wide green leaves, the flowers' small bells would bring a soft whiteness to the shady area at the foot of the stone wall, where a fern already grows.

Rescue is a wonderful excuse for theft. Then, my friend Karen, the folklorist, gives me another reason. She has traveled to Denmark, where she asked a master gardener about Not-Thanking. The gardener had indeed heard of the custom and added, "Furthermore, if you admire a plant in someone's garden, the best way to get a piece for growing in one's own garden is to steal it. Pinch a leaf and steal it away." Karen also tells me that there are ethical standards for plant-stealing: helping yourself to a cutting is perfectly acceptable, for a plant grown from a stolen cutting is said to root better than if it's given, but if you want to dig something up, it's best to get the owner's permission beforehand. Alas, I cannot pinch off a leaf when it comes to purloining plants from the Luddites, for the things that I covet cannot be grown from pinched-off cuttings. Springing up from bulbs or rhizomes, they all require digging. Rescue, I keep telling myself, that's all the rationale needed.

Plants that volunteer bring surprise upon surprise, an aspect of Garden that generates much pleasure and just as much infuriation. Where do they come from, these importuning upstarts? I do know that some sow themselves from seeds or seedlings that were planted in preceding springs. Petite marigolds always pop up in the wooden planter in the front yard. Zinnias do the same in the backyard around the currant bushes. Once, in the same spot, a red-flowered impatiens resurrected itself, although that's not something to be expected in a climate that usually features winter temperatures in the teens and many feet of snow. But the annual cosmos (*Cosmos bipinnatus*) don't mind the winters here. Come spring, they sprout in all the grassless patches out in back. Sometimes I yank, sometimes I let them stay.

The volunteers that produce a summer's worth of pure delight are the sunflowers (*Helianthus annuus*) in the vegetable garden—sunflowers of many dispositions, tall, short, single-blossomed, and multi-flowering. Their origin is obvious and leads herewith to a precept:

Place the pole that holds bird feeders in the middle of the vegetable patch. Come spring, strewn seeds will sprout, and in summer the flowers will open wide their great golden eyes. Let them stay in the garden after the seeds form, and they'll be visited often by feasting chickadees, titmice, and finches.

Let the birds do the work of planting. I admit, however, to helping out by scattering packaged seeds at four-week intervals. That method makes for a variety of colors—not only yellow but also rust and red flowers amid the furry green leaves—and petal patterns that may be as extravagant as those of dahlias. Some plants have multiple flowers, not just a big one at the top but also smaller blooms that sprout from the junctures of leaves and stem. Sunflowers may be cut, too, and brought inside to add their glowing light to kitchen, living room, or front hall.

And willy-nilly, trees spring up. Just as the killer black walnut was surely an unwitting gift from a nut-burying squirrel, the red mulberry, *Morus rubra*, must have arrived in the yard via a seed-excreting bird. I welcomed that mulberry at first. Growing discreetly by the fence on the south side of the backyard, it not only offered shade but also food for both the birds and me. Memory of the berries' seductive sweetness lingered from my childhood. Those long-ago trees figured as ornamental plantings along the front drive of the Virginia School for the Deaf and the Blind, located ten houses down from my grandmother's house. In the summertime, the students were out of school; so, my friends and I had the fruit all to ourselves. We'd strap on our roller skates and zip down to the school grounds. Then, skates doffed, we'd stand under laden branches that drooped like a willow's almost to the ground and enclosed us in a dappled light. Oh, we stuffed ourselves. By the time we'd finished gorging, we were stained all over with purple juice—faces, necks, hands, clothing. I did savor some fruit from the uninvited mulberry in the backyard, but in those days I was farming and fishing in North Carolina. The mulberry therefore gave much of its bounty to the birds and dropped the rest on the grass. And the tree grew with wild abandon—in its final year, it shot three feet upward and gained girth in its canopy, too. It began to crowd the spiraea, wrap its bark round the meshes of the chain-link fence, and broadcast shade over an increasingly large portion of the yard. That fall, after the Chief and I had made our annual wrong-way migration from south to north, he cut it down. The following year, the neighbor who mowed our grass while we were away tended to the suckers thrusting forth with nearly indomitable vigor. But our neighbor's diligence had greater force: the tree did not resurrect itself in the following year. Elizabeth Lawrence, the notable plantswoman and garden writer, once asked a friend interested in earth and seeds, "Are you cruel enough to be a gardener?" Another garden writer speaks of the guilt that accompanies such cruelty: "It is troubling to decide what shall live and what shall die—to do your best for some flower and to yank another summarily out of the ground." Here at Tomato Haven, we've done in the red mulberry and the black walnut. There's a precept here:

Slaughter is an inescapable part of gardening.

In a poem about a dogwood tree, the poet and a passionate gardener Jeffery Beam has written of the tree that it is a place where "Death & Being exchange vows." The thought applies to all gardens, all green-growing things.

But, oh, another volunteer has appeared in the place where the mulberry once grew—a redbud (*Cercis canadensis*), a tree to cherish. On my first encounter with this upstart, I'd cut it back in an overly exuberant trimming of all the shrubs—forsythia, rose of Sharon, and spiraea—along the chain-link fence. Its heart-shaped leaves were only recognized in afterthought. But the following spring, it sprouted buds on its slender trunk, and not much later the deep pink flowers burst into delicate bloom. An amazing sight—flowers growing right out of a trunk! Only when the flowers had dropped did the tree send forth new branches that were soon decked with leaves that look for all the world like green valentines. Sometimes, redbud is called Judastree, a name that properly belongs to a Mediterranean member of the genus *Cercis*. Legend reports that Judas Iscariot hanged himself on such a tree and that its white flowers turned pink with shame. The American redbud was noted by George Washington and Thomas Jefferson. John Lawson, an Englishman who'd come to the Carolinas, published a book in 1709 listing the American plants and animals that he'd seen. He writes, "The Red-Bud-Tree bears a purple Lark-Heel, and is the best Sallad, of any Flower I ever saw. It is ripe in *April* and *May*." "Lark-Heel" refers to the spur on the small flower. But the thing that caught my attention—and caught it at the right moment, the time of bloom—was the reference to salad. I picked a flower and popped it into my mouth. Mmm, sugar-sweet! The volunteer redbud is certainly a tree to cherish. The problem is that it's also been found desirable by insects—little black critters wearing two red stripes across their backs. Drained of juice by these vegetation vampires, the outermost twigs and leaves droop and die. And herewith, another precept.

If insects plague your plants—or if you see one that simply excites your curiosity, catch it, put it in a plastic zipper bag, and take it to the nearest Agricultural Cooperative Extension Agency. You'll not only get an ID but also information on its habits and how to handle it. This tactic works for weeds, too.

I captured one of the little devils and took it to a master gardener at the cooperative extension. Neither she nor anyone else at hand could identify the insect. It was then carefully picked up by tweezers, deposited into a small plastic tube, and sent to the extension entomologist at Virginia Tech. The answer came back almost overnight: *Prosapia bicincta*, less formally known as the two-lined spittlebug. The report says that it can be done in with chemicals like Sevin but that it's "rarely of economic importance." In this case, bug-slaughter is unnecessary because most of the redbud is not afflicted.

But in the matter of green-growing things, from grass to tree to weed to overgrown thyme to droopy tomato, nothing is immune to slaughter, and not just by my hand. The reasons for culling plants from the garden are many. Sometimes there's simply too much of a good thing, especially herbs; they're dug up, put in pots, and given away. Sometimes a plant is moribund, like the wilting tomato that's been attacked by fungi, or the green beans that have ended production. The aggressive nature of both walnut and mulberry had to be dealt with if we wanted other, gentler plants to flourish. But I've waged—and still wage—all-out war against the ailanthus (*Ailanthus altissima*).

Imprecations upon the ailanthus! Scattering its seeds with indecent lavishness or readily shooting up clones from its roots, the tree commandeers space with a notable ruthlessness. And it stinks. When torn—and tearing them is all too easy—the leaves emit a horrid musk, somewhere between rotten eggs and skunk. To think that this takeover artist's name, a latinizing of a language spoken in the Mollucas, means "tree of heaven"! And altissima means "the highest." It's really a species spawned in hell. It's also the tree featured in Betty Smith's novel *A Tree Grows in Brooklyn*. If only it had confined itself to Brooklyn. If only it had not been imported in the first place from China. The first ailanthus arrived in America in 1784 by way of one William Hamilton, who planted it on his estate just outside Philadelphia. Hamilton had seen the tree growing in the garden of Louis XVI's physician. Told that it had been grown from seed sent to France in 1751 by a missionary and that it was exceedingly rare, Hamilton lusted for an ailanthus of his own. The tree that he brought home was much admired, and one thing led to another. By 1820, the species was being imported for sale and much promoted as a suitable component of the landscaping of estates and parks. It was then that New York began to use it as a street tree; other cities, including Philadelphia and Washington, D.C., followed suit. Nor was it planted only in metropolises but was also cultivated in the countryside because its wood proved useful for fencing and fireplaces. But as a botanical historian has written:

> By midcentury [1850], the tree of heaven had spread of its own volition from Massachusetts to the Mississippi, and from the Deep South to Texas. But its very vigor undermined its popularity. Cities found the maturing trees difficult to control. Their insistent spreading roots sent volunteer trees up through sidewalks and the foundations of buildings, and along roadsides where nobody wanted them. When they began to bloom, millions of inchworms dropped from them onto pedestrians, and many people were allergic to their pollen.

The damn tree is still everywhere. I note especially dense stands along the sides of Interstate 64. But it's still widely admired because it accepts urban conditions, resists pollution, and lacks fussiness about the soil in which it grows. And the botanical historian writes that in spring, "Where no other green thing can thrive, its great fronds of leaves provide shade and beauty." Shade and beauty, indeed! Obviously, she has never lived with an ailanthus in her backyard. But if I allowed the tree to gain a foothold here, it would exterminate the grass all by itself. Nothing but ailanthus would be left. My onetime landlord, whose wife snitched my tomatoes, came to the rescue. He gave me a bottle filled with a blue herbicide, Pathway, which is widely used by forestry people. It had gotten him into considerable trouble with a next-door neighbor, whose backyard (just to the west of my onetime tomato patch) was solidly overgrown with sixty-foot ailanthus trees. Acting as their kind does, they had sent runners under the fence into my landlord's territory. At that, he cut the intruders down and painted the stumps blue with Pathway. Behold, the neighbor's ailanthus drooped and died, whereupon an insurance claim was filed. My landlord's homeowner's policy anted up almost two thousand dollars in recompense for trash trees—murdered trash trees, but trash trees nonetheless. Pathway and a disposable foam brush at hand, I have sawed and painted. The problem is now under control though certainly not cleared up, for the Luddites encourage not only bur cucumber but also a sizeable stand of ailanthus that grows brashly behind their shed. But if it dies, I doubt that they'll notice.

The garden grows—and grows and grows, not just organically but with objects. Some are practical; and others, ornamental. The latter are often objects that I would not have acquired on my own. In fact, some of them are cutesy or downright tacky. One of them is a plastic sapsucker on a wire stake; when the breezes blow, its wings whirl around and around, making an audible clatter. It's on display in the front yard between the tarragon and the dusty miller. Another front-yard object, which reposes beside the front walk, is a large, curly-haired gray cat made of plaster; in its mouth it holds a scaly fish, and from the fish dangles a plaque reading WELCOME. Despite the fact that they are kitsch, getting rid of these items is out of the question, for a friend gave me the whirly bird, and a granddaughter, the cat. I appreciate completely the sentiments behind the gifts. You do thank people for such things, and to throw them away would be tantamount to withdrawing the thanks.

Several of the inorganic contributions to my garden's well-being have brought pure delight. A stepping stone molded with a dragonfly in low relief rests in the earth next to the cat. A sandhill crane made of metal and almost as tall as the real thing stands amid ferns in front of the limestone wall; in the morning sunlight, it casts an elegant shadow twice as big as itself. Dragonfly came from a friend, and the crane, from a cousin. A birdhouse, built by another cousin, is suspended from a pole-mounted steel bracket that was crafted by my son. Its presence prompts another precept:

Place a birdhouse near the vegetable patch. There shall be music as you pick the beans and harvest the tomatoes.

The house has been inhabited by house wrens. Their nest of twigs filled the box right up to its round opening. I saw the female ducking in and out while the male perched on the hanger or on the Norway spruce to sing his heart out. My heart took wing.

HERBS

A little madness in the Spring
Is wholesome even for the King,
But God be with the Clown,
Who ponders this tremendous scene—
This whole experiment of green,
As if it were his own!

—*Emily Dickinson, XXXVIII*

THE GARDEN'S FIRST GREEN HARVEST ARRIVES QUIETLY in the front yard at the end of March and, by mid-April, can't be stopped: the perennial herbs—thyme, creeping rosemary, winter savory, oregano, chives, sage, and tarragon. For the next two months, until the middle of June, I pick leaves and cut slender branches to put in the dehydrator. And, oh, my kitchen is filled with the infinitely varied scents of the green world! Jar on jar fills with aromatic crumbles, some used for everyday cooking and some put aside as house presents or Christmas gifts. Summer heat brings on the tiny blossoms that lure bees and skippers to their nectar. After flowering, the quality drops off, for the plants devote their attention to producing seed rather than the essential oils that give each one its distinctive flavor. You may want to know why basil is absent from this list. The reason is that it's an annual, which I start from seed and plant along with the carrots in the backyard's raised bed.

Herbs are surely the most economical edibles that anyone can grow. For one, they take up very little room. You can easily make a container garden for herbs, using small pots that may be brought inside when cold weather arrives. Outside, a four-by-four-foot bed supplies all the room that's needed. I do not, however, put herbs into a bed of their own but mix them up with the front yard's gaillardia, black-eyed Susans, and sedums. For two, because many of the herbs I've listed form carpets, weeds are kept to a minimum. For three, bottled herbs bought at the grocery story are purse-busters; one .62-ounce jar of tarragon costs as much all by itself as a two-person meal of meatloaf, mashed potatoes, and green beans. But herb seeds are not expensive, nor are the started plants that you can buy at farmers' markets. As for jars, here's a precept:

Save your glass herb and spice jars, and ask your friends to do the same. They can be happily recycled. But beware of plastic jars, for they may retain the odors and flavors of their former contents.

A dehydrator is not an expensive item. Using one saves time, for it dries herbs speedily. But you may choose to hang cut stems upside down in a dry place. Another method involves laying the stems flat on the kind of cardboard tray that nurseries and garden centers provide for transporting plants and then placing the tray or trays on the backseat of a closed-up car that sits in the late spring sun. Within two or three days, the interior heat will dissipate every last bit of moisture in the leaves.

My garden's herbs come from a variety of sources: transplant, gift, purchase, and packets of seeds. But before I go into the details, it may be well to introduce you more fully to one of my chief garden consultants, John Gerard (1545–1612), an English botanist, who published a list of the plants growing in his garden in 1597. Describing more than 1,000 species that are illustrated with almost twice that many woodcuts, his *Herball* is packed with folklore and notes on the medicinal uses of the plants, as well as copious notes on their appearances and habits of growth. The 1633 revision of this monumental book—it's as large as an unabridged dictionary—was republished in the United States in 1975. It shall be cited often in the pages that follow.

✒ OREGANO (*ORIGANUM VULGARE*)

What would homemade spaghetti sauce be without oregano? What, stewed tomatoes? What, pizza? Just as there are companion plantings in the garden, there are companion flavors in the kitchen. Tomatoes and oregano are just such a twosome. I've grown the herb for at least a dozen years now. Way back when, it arrived in my North Carolina yard as a house present, and it came north with me when I moved back to Tomato Haven full-time. It has burgeoned here ever since.

Like many herbs, oregano is one of the Lamiaceae, the Mints, a family well endowed with essential oils that give them distinctive flavors and aromas. This herb's name gives away its origin in the Mediterranean, for *origanum* is the latinization of an ancient Greek word meaning "mountain-joy," most likely for the wild plant's favored habitat. *Vulgare* translates simply as "common." Its earliest uses seem to have been ceremonial and, more important, medicinal. Myth describes it as a gift from Aphrodite, and when they married, bride and groom might wreathe their heads with oregano. Pliny, the Roman naturalist of the first century A.D., calls the herb a necessary item in the Roman pharmacopoeia, and so does his contemporary Dioscorides, a Greek who served as surgeon to Nero's troops and wrote extensively on the materia medica obtained from plants. John Gerard calls it organy, wild marjoram, or bastard marjoram. And, indeed, it shares its genus with marjoram, *Origanum majorana*, "mountain-joy marjoram," though marjoram is not nearly so powerful, for it lacks the phenolic compounds that give oregano its zing. And, oh, the virtues of oregano, according to Gerard! Here is a far from complete sampling of his list of its medical powers:

> Organy given in wine is a remedy against the bitings and stingings of venomous beasts, and cureth them that have drunke Opium.
> The decoction of Organy provoketh urine, bringeth down the monthly course, and is given with good successe to those that have the dropsie.
> It healeth scabs, itches, and scurvinesse, being used in bathes, and it taketh away the bad colour which cometh of the yellow jaundice.
> The juice mixed with a little milke, being poured into the ears, mitigateth the paines thereof.

So, the sauce that covers our spaghetti fends off all manner of ills, from bee stings to menstrual pain.

The quality of homegrown oregano can vary widely. In northern climates, especially those that are damp, it loses its pungency. One authority on herbs writes, "The plant as it grows wild in southern Italy is a far more violent herb even than that which grows in northern Italy. Herewith' a precept:

When you buy plants or seed, make sure that you get the cultivar known as Greek oregano, Origanum vulgare hirtum, *sometimes known as* O. heracleoticum. *It will have the proper violence.*

Dried oregano is more flavorful than fresh. So, dry it in a dehydrator or the backseat of your car.

⚜ SAGE (*SALVIA OFFICINALIS*)

Sage, with its lovely gray-green or variegated leaves, is also a member of the Lamiaceae, the Mints. Its genus-name comes from the Latin word *salvere*, "to heal," in testimony to its long-standing medicinal use. The species-name means "sold in shops" for medicinal and culinary purposes. The sage that we use in cooking is native to the Mediterranean and Asia Minor and has been grown in northern Europe since the Middle Ages, but other members of its genus are also found in the New World. Central America is home to several species, including pineapple and peach sages (*S. rutilans* and *S. greggi* respectively), and it is there that the one and only hallucinogenic species in the Mint family is found—*S. divinorum*, "sage of the gods."

John Gerard has much, of course, to say about the uses of sage. He writes: "Sage is singular good for the head and braine; it quickeneth the senses and memory, strengthneth the sinews, restoreth health to those that have the palsie, takes away shaking or trembling of the members; and being put up into the nostrils, it draweth thin flegme out of the head." His list contains six more equally long descriptions of sage's curative powers, including preventing spontaneous abortions, warding off the effects of snakebite, and healing cold sores.

I place my faith not in sage's purported ability to heal but in its flavors. Because its leathery leaves do not dry well, I chop and freeze it. Put later into a skillet with butter, it's sizzled for half a minute before chicken is added for browning. I also put it, along with fresh diced onions, into the ordinary poultry stuffing from the grocery store. Or, with oregano, thyme, basil, and savory, it's added to a stick of butter, which is softened and mashed. The flavored butter is slathered on sliced Italian or French bread, which is then wrapped in foil and baked until the butter melts. Behold, herb bread.

⚜ WINTER SAVORY (*SATUREJA MONTANA*)

Winter savory, the formal name of which translates as "mountain savory," also belongs to the Lamiaceae, the Mints, as does its close cousin summer savory (*S. hortensis,* "garden savory"). Both probably originated in western or central Asia but early found their way to the Mediterranean. Garden savory is somewhat less pungent, and it's the species found (if found at all) on grocery-store spice shelves, but it's a half-hardy annual. By contrast, winter savory is perennial. The fact that it overwinters easily is the reason that it grows in my garden, rather than its more tender genus-mate.

Bohnenkraut, "bean-plant," is the German name for winter savory, for often it was cooked along with beans and other legumes. John Gerard credits it with reducing the flatulence occasioned by eating beans. Because of its peppery flavor, it has been used as a poor-man's pepper, though it does not really do the job. Best to use it fresh in salads or herb butter.

Winter savory needs little care. I clip it back come fall so that new spring leaves are not overshadowed. Then, in late spring, when it's in takeover mode, reaching out and putting down roots way past its bounds, I dig up portions and pot them. The potted plants make marvelous gifts. I hand them out as house presents and also as souvenirs to passersby, many of them strangers, who stop to chat as they walk past the garden.

ROSEMARY (*ROSMARINUS OFFICINALIS*)

Here's yet another of the Lamiaceae, the Mints, one known for its resinous piney-woods scent. Its formal name means "dew of the sea that's sold in shops," likely because the plant, a shrub, grows profusely in the countries that surround the Mediterranean. It has served all sorts of purposes. Rosemary has long symbolized friendship and remembrance. Then, it has been thought to have power over the forces of evil: sprigs were tucked under medieval pillows to ward off witches and nightmares. In the sixteenth century, rich people hired perfumers to come into their houses and heat rosemary over hot coals to fill a house with its scent. It was taken north into monastery gardens not for cooking purposes but as a simple used in traditional medicine. The only culinary applications for rosemary that John Gerard mentions is that it "is spice in Germane kitchins, and other cold countries" and that its sugared flowers when eaten "comfort the heart, and make it merry." But, far more interested in its other uses, he notes that so much of it grows in Languedoc that people there use it as firewood, and that it's planted as hedging in England and Italy. He advises us that "Rosemarie is a remedie against the stuffing of the head, that commeth through coldness of the brain, if a garland thereof be put about the head." If only getting rid of the common cold were that simple! Gerard also informs us that drinking water in which rosemary flowers have been steeped will sweeten bad breath.

I've also heard it said that the possession of a rosemary shrub of large size indicates that a woman dominates the household. That's the kind of shrub that I grew in North Carolina—huge. Brought as a gift by one of the birders who traipsed regularly through our riverside yard, it began its life with me as a rooted sprig no taller than my little finger. The next spring, I was amazed to see that it had survived in fine, perky shape. The year after, it had turned itself into a good-sized bush and, the year after that, had attained a diameter of some eight feet and a height of five. Spring and fall, delicate flowers of pale purple-blue decked the branches. A story has it that the flowers were once white but turned blue when the Virgin Mary hung her robe on a bush as she fled with her son from Herod's army. When I made my final migration north, I brought cuttings, rooted them, and planted them in the backyard (the front did not have space enough to accommodate a giant shrub). But they did not live. The reason is that my northern plant-hardiness zone is 6, while that of coastal North Carolina is a far warmer 8. Rosemary, though perennial, is subject to frost-kill. Here, I must replace it annually. And I buy the creeping sort that hugs the ground rather than turning into a huge bush. Against all expectations, the enormous rosemary of my former life still thrives. I'd thought that the havoc of Hurricane Isabel in 2003 would have taken it away. Isabel devasted my old Carolina neighborhood, wrecking seawalls, inundating houses, and completely demolishing the mobile home in which the Chief and I had spent eighteen splendid years. But when I went south to visit friends, I made a trip to my former haunts: the great rosemary stood in the yard as sassy as ever, a true green survivor.

Rosemary is a survivor in other respects. The plant in my yard is tame, acquired at the farmers' market, but others of its kind have escaped into the wild. It has naturalized itself on both coasts of the United States and may be found in California, Oregon, North Carolina, South Carolina, and Puerto Rico.

Unlike many herbs, rosemary does not lose its flavor after long cooking. And it works as well dried as fresh. I find that it suits potatoes. Cutting unpeeled potatoes into wedges, I mix in a coarsely diced onion, rosemary leaves, and enough olive oil to coat the potatoes. Roast for 30 minutes at 425°. The rosemary-'taters make a fit companion for everything from chicken to fish.

⚘ THYME (*THYMUS VULGARIS*)

Common thyme, a perennial sometimes called garden thyme, is still another of the Lamiaceae, the Mint family. It's native to the Mediterranean. The name of its genus comes from the ancient Greek word *thymos*, meaning "spirit" or "soul," which has been latinized to *thymus*. It may also be related to the Greek word for "fumigate." Once upon a time, it was indeed used to smoke stinging insects out of a house, and its dried flowers have been used to repel insects that infest linen. But some of the earliest records that we have of thyme attest to its attractiveness to bees. Virgil, advising on the plantings best put near beehives, writes:

> Let green and fragrant laurel flower all around—wild thyme,
>   as well,
> broadcasting its perfume, and much strong-smelling savory.

He also mentions "thyme-scented honey," famous in the ancient world and equally relished today.

A herb with such a powerful odor naturally acquired a host of medicinal uses. According to Gerard, thyme—"Time" as he spells it—was a powerful medicine that helped both mind and body. Boiled in water and honey, it calmed coughing. Made into a powder and mixed with honeyed vinegar, it cured sciatica and eased those who were "fearefull, melancholike, and troubled in minde." Sniffed, it alleviated epilepsy. Like rosemary and many other potent herbs, thyme actually does possesses antibacterial and antifungal properties, which aid in food preservation by impeding or killing the microorganisms that often cause spoilage in food. As late as World War I, its most prominent essential oil, thymol, was used as a wound-cleansing antiseptic.

Some species and cultivars of thyme come with unconventional scents and flavors. Would you like caraway? Try *T. herba-barona*, which uses the Corsican word for the plant as its species-name. How about orange? That one's *T. vulgaris odoratissimus*, sometimes known as *T. fragrantissimus*. As for lemon thyme, it's a hybrid, *T. pulegioides* x *T. vulgaris* (*pulegoides* means "like pennyroyal"). But I prefer plain common thyme for cooking and find that its dried form is entirely satisfactory. It's an ingredient, sine qua non, to soups, herb bread, and meatloaf.

But to my way of thinking, the most enchanting use of thyme is to plant a patch in the garden as a green carpet beneath the leaves of which fairies may make themselves at home. The fairies represent the garden's green energy, of course. Later, I'll have a great deal more to say on this vital subject.

CHIVES (*ALLIUM SCHOENOPRASUM*)

My chive plant made the journey up from North Carolina in its pot, where, set on a paving stone near the front steps, it has flourished ever since. It may be well to explain right now why the word "chive" is singular: that form refers to the plant, while the plural, "chives," belongs to the leaves. The growing plant is linguistically one thing; the leaves, cut and chopped, quite another. No matter which you're talking about, this perennial herb belongs to the Liliaceae, the Lily family, and the binomial means "rush-leek onion," a name that recognizes the similarity of its slender, hollow leaves to those of rushes. The word "chive" comes from the Latin word for onion, *cepa*, which softened to *cive* in Old French. No one knows chive's point of origin, but it is likely to have been central Asia or the Far East. The plants migrated to Europe in ancient times and came to the New World much later with the colonists.

What are they good for? It's said that they promote appetite and aid digestion. I savor the flavor, which is far better if the leaves are fresh, not dried. Use chopped chives or whole leaves to garnish potatoes or spicy cauliflower soup (for the latter, see page 127–128). Put chopped chives into garden or potato salads. Stir them into sour cream. One of chive's virtues is that it can easily be grown year-round in a pot. Before a black frost strikes, bring the pot inside and place it in a sunny window. If it's left outside, frost will kill the leaves, of course, but when a warm spell comes in January, encouraging the daffodils and summer snowflakes to thrust up the tips of their leaves, a chive plant will also sprout new greenery. Come summer, I let the plant bloom for a while before cutting it back. The flowers, soft lavender puffs, are beautiful.

᪥ TARRAGON (*ARTEMISIA DRACUNCULUS*)

"Little dragon sacred to the goddess Artemis"—that's the meaning of the binomial for this perennial plant. "Dragon" refers to the snaky appearance of its root, which John Gerard describes as "long and fibrous, creeping far abroad under the earth." Indeed, one French term for the plant is *herbe dragone*, "dragon herb." Like the sunflower and the marigold, it belongs to the Asteraceae, the Aster family. As for its origins, there's some disagreement. One usually authoritative Internet source gives its native habitat as central Asia, probably Siberia, while the U.S. Department of Agriculture's Plants Database says that it's native to North America and grows in the wild in all of the contiguous states west of the Mississippi, plus Alaska. I cannot know for certain, but it may be that the plant was brought over the land bridge that once linked Siberia and Alaska. That was the route by which people entered the New World and the horses left. At any rate, tarragon has dozens of relatives in North America; it shares its genus with many native species of sagebrush, sagewort, and wormwood. Other artemesias are native to the Old World; one of them is the notorious *A. absinthium*, which provides thujone, one of the essential oils that flavors absinthe and is as intoxicating as marijuana, a fact that has caused this green liquor to be banned in the U.S.

Tarragon, often known in the U.S. as French tarragon, intoxicates only by its sensuousness—its anise flavor and scent. Wherever the herb originated, it was known in Europe before the turn of the century from B.C. to A.D. The Roman naturalist Pliny prescribed it to prevent fatigue, and pilgrims in the Middle Ages put it in their shoes to keep from getting tired on their long treks to various points of worship. Uncharacteristically, Gerard says nothing of its medicinal uses and notes only that it's a good salad herb. He does, however, repeat a rumor about the plant that was spread in the 1530s by the botanist Ruellius, who translated the book on medicinal plants written in Latin the first century A.D. by the physician and pharmacologist Dioscorides: "*Ruellius* and such others have reported many strange tales hereof scarce worth the noting, saying, that the seed of flaxe put into a radish roote or sea Onion, and so set, doth bring forth this herbe Tarragon." But Gerard knew better. I'm surprised, though, that he says nothing about one peculiar property of the herb: if you pop a fresh leaf in your mouth and chew, your tongue will tingle and briefly turn numb.

If you wish to grow tarragon, best to take (steal!) a cutting and root it or buy a plant; seed does not always produce a desirable variety. When it comes to using the herb for culinary purposes, some guides advise using it fresh rather than dried, but I have found the latter entirely satisfactory in such dishes as chicken cooked in broth with diced onions and an ample sprinkling of tarragon. For flavoring vinegar, however, nothing but fresh will do. And the making of vinegar involves a precept:

> *Save old vinegar bottles of clear or light-colored glass for making herb vinegars. Dark glass won't do because it conceals the branch put within, and seeing the herb, stem, and leaves is part of this enterprise's charm.*

Once again, the garden provides things to keep and give away.

❧ BASIL (*OCIMUM BASILICUM*)

Basil brings me back to the Lamiaceae, the Mint family. The formal name of this annual means "king's herb," with *Ocimum* being a latinization of a classical Greek word that referred to an aromatic herb that may—or may not—have been basil. Its aroma and flavor are fit for a king, not to mention a commoner. Native to India, Asia, and Africa, it has made its way around the world. What would Italian cooking be without *pesto* and French, without *pistou*, both dependent on the royal herb?

Much lore is connected with basil, particularly in connection with romance. Once upon a time in France, a pot of basil set on a woman's balcony signaled that she was ready to receive a suitor. And a sprig of basil given by a man to a woman was sure to make her fall in love with him. It also symbolized fertility. On the other hand, its name conflated with "basilisk," a legendary reptile with lethal breath, basil was also thought by some southern Europeans to be able to produce scorpions if its crushed leaves were put between two bricks. Noting that some writers say that "the smell of Basill is good for the heart and for the head," John Gerard also reports some disapprobation: "*Dioscorides* saith that if Basil be much eaten, it dulleth the sight, it mollifieth the belly, breedeth winde, provoketh urine, drieth up milke, and is of hard digestion." Gerard himself rather approves of it, citing the herb as a remedy for headache and dim eyesight. It also cheers the melancholic.

Nor does the lore cease here. There is John Keats's famous poem, "Isabella; or, The Pot of Basil," which versifies a truly gruesome tale from Boccaccio. Isabella's true love, Lorenzo, was killed and buried in the depths of a forest by her brothers. Missing him, she waited in vain for his return. But he came to her in a vision, asked her to find his grave, and there shed one tear to console him. Isabella and her ancient nurse did succeed in finding the corpse, whereupon they cut off his head and took it home, where it was placed in a pot of basil. Watered by her tears, the plant thrived until her murderous brothers stole the pot. At that, heartsick, stricken, Isabella died.

There's one thing wrong with this scenario: basil does not like overwatering, even with tears. It rejoices in sun and rich soil. I start seeds in the cold frame and transplant them into the raised bed when there is no danger of frost. The variety that I most often plant is large-leaved Genovese basil; occasionally, the cultivar 'Purple Ruffles' joins it. Green or purple, the taste is the same. *O. basilicum* also comes in cultivars with cinnamon and anise flavors, and the species *O. americanum*, "American herb," has a lemony tang. There's one more species that needs mentioning, *O. sanctum*, "holy herb," which is sacred in India and dedicated to the gods Vishnu and Krishna. During the days of the British raj in India, Hindus, who have no bible, swore on this basil, which they called *tulsi*, to tell the truth, the whole truth, and nothing but the truth. Though it's not used in cooking, it makes a lovely ornamental plant, and seeds are available from seed companies.

To preserve basil for future use, I mince and freeze it, and I also dry it. Books specializing in such matters do not recommend the latter method because basil supposedly loses its flavor after a few weeks in a jar. For making pesto out of season, use the frozen leaves. But for adding to spaghetti sauce and stewed tomatoes or sprinkling liberally in tomato soup, the dried variety will do the job. And when basil is in the dehydrator, it fills my kitchen with its joyful green scent.

Other herbs have found room in my garden, among them two of the Umbelliferae, the Carrot family, so named because of their ferny leaves. One is the annual, liberally self-seeding cilantro, *Coriandrum sativum*, which means "cultivated coriander"; the other is the biennial parsley, *Petroselinum crispum*, "closely curled rock-parsley," no matter that the variety I grow is the superbly flavorful Italian sort with large, flat leaves. Like basil, parsley is best preserved by freezing. As for cilantro, the difference between its leaves and fruit is astonishing. I eschew the soapy-flavored leaves and wait until the plant reaches the coriander stage, when it produces little round seeds redolent of oranges. On occasion, I grow another annual member of the Carrot family—dill, *Anethum graveolens*, "heavily scented dill," which is wonderful when used fresh on cooked cabbage, but I usually let the plants go to seed and put the fruits in a jar after they've dried naturally. One herb with which I have had no success—but for good reason—is catnip, a perennial Mint-family member, *Nepeta cataria*, "cat's ground-ivy." I cannot grow it inside, for it would be ravaged by my two cats, both of which are addicts, but when I tried to grow it outside, it was fair game for the neighborhood's semiferal junkies. Borage, *Borago officinalis*, "borage sold in shops," was another experiment. The pale blue flowers of this annual are a joy (and said to be delicious in salad), but the plants grow so tall—some three feet—that they easily flop over. I may well plant it again, however, for it's reputed to be a good companion plant for strawberries. I'll need to keep an eye on it though, for one encyclopedia warns that it "must remain the junior partner."

Lavender deserves a paragraph of its own. A perennial member of the Mint family, it's formally *Lavandula angustifolia*, "narrow-leaved lavender," with the word "lavender" coming from the Latin *lavere*, "to wash." Time out of mind, this native of the Mediterranean has been used to perfume soaps and bathwater. It was the favorite scent of the no-nonsense grandmother for whom I am named, and

the plant grows in her honor amid the other herbs in the front garden. Its gray-green leaves, its small purple flowers, and its sweet scent
bring memories of my growing-up days when my mother, brothers,
and I lived in her house during World War II, when my father was
gone for a soldier. Lavender has long been associated with love; for
me, it signals remembrance.

Gerard's comment that basil is good for the heart and good for
the head applies to all the herbs in my garden. More than that,
they're good for the eyes and for the tongue, amen.

FLOWERS

Some garden plants, such as asters or
primroses, come in forms
or cultivars too numerous
for most of us;
choosing among them is what
makes your garden
different from mine or
someone else's.

—*Suzanne McIntyre,*
An American Cutting Garden

DAYLILIES

T HE CHOICES THAT I'VE MADE AMONG FLOWERS have given
my garden a certain panache, the gaudier the better. Sedum
pink clashes with cayenne red and marigold orange. Delicate
lavender abuts daylily peach and plum. It's flowers that contribute
most of the garden's colors other than green. But choosing among
them not only makes each garden different but also presents enough
difficulties and confusion to make your head spin—annual or
perennial, ground-hugging plants or high-risers, red, pink, or yellow, and in what combinations? One visitor, a down-on-her-knees,
back-to-the-earth sort of gardener, looked at the colors in my front
yard—silver-gray dusty miller next to a variegated geranium with
red blooms that is in turn set next to a pert gray-green sedum that
flourishes beside the tiny, red-leaved Japanese maple, and she said
somewhat sadly, "Leaves are supposed to be green." I cannot disagree, but they're also supposed to be anything else that's in their

genes. The maple can't help its red leaves or the dusty miller its frosted foliage any more than I can help having hazel eyes and gray hair. Suffice it to say that her garden is not a bit like mine.

My garden is a muddle, mixing flowers with herbs, vegetables, shrubs, and trees. (The weeds will have their turn in another chapter.) I like these combinations because for me they optimize the possibilities for color, produce, and—most of all—delight. If there's a theme, it is exuberance. Out with tidiness! In with plants that elbow and jostle one another and proclaim their joy by erupting with blossoms and fruit! Some flowers are dependable, others persnickity. Often, experimentation offers the only way to determine which is benevolent, and which as temperamental as a two-year-old.

DAYLILIES (*HEMEROCALLIS*)

I have favorites, of course, and chief among them are the daylilies. They come in an extraordinary range of colors, from gold and apricot to flamingo pink and burgundy, not to mention insouciant roadside orange. If the yard at Tomato Haven were twice its size, half would be devoted to these flowers with a scientific name that translates to "beauties of a day." The blossoms open in the morning and are gone by evening. But the scapes—the stems, that is—may be cut for arrangements because they bear a number of buds; when one folds, another opens.

The first daylilies that I remember grew in my grandmother's backyard garden. Set on one of the town's steep hills, it sloped downward in three terraces, connected by stone steps. On the highest, she'd planted a rock garden. The next two, grassy in the center, were surrounded by flower beds. Flowers other than daylilies must have grown there, but only the daylilies made an impression. They were daylilies of the most ordinary sort—no burgundies or whites with deep red throats, just orange and yellow. I thought, literally, that they were sweet. And when they bloomed, my friends and I needed not one or two but dozens to give us a sugar fix. We would ravage the lilies, pulling off the blossoms and sucking the nectar out at the stem ends. With hindsight, I can now realize that the yard must have looked as if it had been struck by a highly selective hurricane that had strewn hundreds of yellow and orange flowers at random over the grass. I know now that my grandmother had grieved at beauty wantonly destroyed. I knew at the time that she was exceeding wroth and that she would punish me. Her punishment was cruel indeed: she scissored out another chunk of my beloved, doll-shaped stuffed rabbit that I clothed in frilly dresses from the five-and-ten and took to bed every night. When I finally outgrew the need for that comforting animal, it had suffered partial amputations of its limbs, and its long, floppy ears were scalloped. I will say on my grandmother's behalf that after each surgery, she always sewed up my rabbit. I have not since felt an urge to sip daylily nectar.

But now, daylilies delight my eyes and spirit. I understand my grandmother's passion for their kind. And they are hardy, withstanding all sorts of harsh treatment. I recall the daylilies that my mother mailed to me in a shoebox four decades ago. They looked desiccated beyond redemption when I opened the package. I planted them anyhow—behold! abundant roadside-orange flowers the following spring. The lemon-yellow and double orange daylilies now growing in my front yard were lifted back in the early '80s from my mother's Virginia garden and planted near our North Carolina waterfront. They exemplify the species' ability to survive truly catastrophic events. Five times they were drowned in salt water that had been hurled ashore by hurricane winds, and five times they rose to bloom again. Now that they've been brought back to the Shenandoah Valley, snows, heavy rains, and sultry summertime heat do not faze them, and they are highly resistant to nibbling, gnawing animals and insects. They flourish, and they spread so vigorously that in a year or two, I'll have daylilies to spare, a fact that leads to a precept:

Growing enough to give away—that's one of a gardener's greatest joys. Nor do you need to plan for extras in the case of lilies, iris, and many other flowers. They spread all by themselves. The gardener's secret here is vigilance so that they're kept within bounds.

Daylilies are members of the Liliaceae, the Lily family, which includes a huge number of plants, many of which grow not from seeds but from bulbs, tubers, corms, and rhizomes. The daylily has a tough fibrous root. Other members of the family include daffodils, tulips, *Kniphofia* or red-hot poker, Oriental lilies (*Lilium* species), and onions. The daylily is a cousin to the wild garlic that I cannot eradicate from the front yard and so use in cooking. Daylilies, as it happens, are also good to eat. They originated in central China, where they were planted in fields so that the buds and flowers would afford a ready supply of both food and medicine. It was thought that the buds, made into a powder, could ameliorate pain and grief and also assure the birth of a son if the powder was worn in a sash around the belly during pregnancy. Nor were people the only beneficiaries: cattle could forage on the green leaves. Such a valuable source of food and pharmaceutical simples could hardly be left at home; so, it traveled the silk roads to eastern Europe. But it did not make its way to western Europe until about 1500; there it was strictly an ornamental plant rather than one with practical applications. Calling it *Lilium non bulbosum Phoeniceum*, "Orange Lily without a bulb," John Gerard describes in his *Herball* the behavior of its "Orenge tawny colour" flowers:

This plant bringeth forth in the morning his bud, which at noone is full blowne, or spred abroad, and the same day in the evening it shuts itself, and in a short time becomes as rotten and stinking as if it had been trodden in a dunghill a moneth together, in foule

and rainie weather: which is the cause that the seed seldome follows, as in the others of his kind, not bringing forth any at all that
I could ever observe; according to the old proverbe, Soone ripe,
soone rotten.

Nonetheless, he admired daylilies and grew them in his garden with
other "fine and rare plants." But despite his observation that they do
not set seed, they do. Egg-shaped green ovals, no bigger around than
my little fingernail, form at the base of the flowers—not many, to be
sure, but always at least one for each bud stalk. Better, however, to
pick off these pods so that the plants do not divert their energies toward making seeds. As for the "rotten and stinking" dunghill smell,
it has eluded me (perhaps because I do not sniff at the spent flowers). But the climate here is far less wet than that of England, and the
flowers on my daylilies simply dry up.

Daylilies came to America with the earliest colonists. By 1695
both orange and yellow daylilies had become well-established from
New England to Virginia. Settlers took them west. And daylilies are
so adaptable that they easily became naturalized in the wild, their
gentle flames brightening roadsides everywhere east of the Mississippi and in many venues to the west—daylilies as wild as their earliest progenitors, which the Chinese domesticated and planted in
fields. But the plants are infinitely amenable to taming, and goodness knows, they're easy to care for:

*Daylilies in the garden require little attention, except
for ardent admiration of their splendid blossoms.
The blossoms do not need deadheading, for they drop
off a day or two after blooming. If seedpods should
form, snip them off. After blooming ceases, cut off the
stems close to earth and cut back the leaves so that
they are only three or four inches high. Within two*

*weeks, the leaves will grow out like slender, fresh
green banners, but not so high as in flowering mode.*

After the leaves are cut back, the earth around the daylilies looks
barren. I go to the drawer in which seed packets are stored and take
out the marigolds.

MARIGOLDS (*TAGETES ERECTA* AND T. *PATULA*)

White, yellow, gold, orange, deep rust-red—marigolds glow with
colors that range from pale noontime sun to flaming evening sunset.
The flowers may be daintily single or extravagantly double, and the
plants with their frilly, finely divided leaves may hug the earth like *T.
patula*, the "spreading marigold," or, like *T. erecta*, the "upright
marigold," rise so tall that they need staking to be kept from toppling
to the ground. Marigolds, though annuals, are vigorous and pushy,
insisting on their right to flourish. And flourish they do, seeding
themselves throughout the growing season, with some seeds over-
wintering to germinate the following spring.

Marigolds belong to the Asteraceae, the Aster family, and it's
mete here to say a few words about the family's name. Its members
are also known the Compositae, the Composite or Daisy family,
but I follow the lead of the U.S. Department of Agriculture, which
has come down firmly on the side of Asteraceae in its database for
this country's plants. The preferred ending for a family name is
-*aceae* (the Mint family, among others, has also undergone this
change; plants once considered part of the Labitiae family are now
the Lamiaceae). The Aster family has worldwide representatives.
But marigolds are strictly a New World phenomenon. The Portuguese found their large-headed yellow flowers in Brazil in the
early 1500s, and Hernán Cortés discovered that these plants with
great sun-gold blossoms were sacred to Mexico's Aztecs. Even now,

Mexican peasants strew graves with marigold petals on All Saints'
Day. Several species, *T. micrantha*, "small-thorned marigold," and
T. lemmonii, "Lemmon's marigold," are native to the American
Southwest and may be found growing wild in Arizona, New Mexico, and Texas. A European taxonomist, however, assigned the
genus-name, which summons an Etruscan deity, Tages, who sprang
from the earth when it was first plowed and, more important, discovered gold. Marigolds definitely display a Tagetian exuberance
and will spring up like bright nuggets even from uncultivated soil.
As for the common name, it belonged in the first place to a golden-
flowered European plant known as the pot marigold (*Calendula officinalis*), and it slipped across the ocean to designate plants that
only resembled those back home. The Portuguese carried the seeds
of the Brazilian marigold to India, the original home of the calendula, which was known there as the herb of the sun and considered
sacred. The New World flowers soon supplanted the calendulas,
and nowadays, a sacred bull will wear a wreath of foreign
marigolds around his neck.

Today, seed catalogues show pictures of French marigolds (*T.
patula*) and African marigolds (*T. erecta*). How did plants native to
the Americas acquire names that seem to place their origins in the
Old World? The tale has to do with transatlantic trade. The Aztecs
provided not just the glorious, giant golden-flowered varieties but
also the dwarf red-and-yellow types. Seeds of the former went to
Spain, where they were planted in monastery gardens, and the
monks sent seeds of these hardy plants to monasteries in France and
North Africa. In North Africa they escaped and made themselves at
home all along the Mediterranean coast from Algeria to Tunisia.
When the Holy Roman emperor Charles V (1500–1558) invaded
North Africa to free several thousand Christian slaves from the
Moors, his eye was caught by "Flos Africanus," the African flower,
and he took its seeds back to Europe, where they were known as
African marigolds until the 1700s.

As for French marigolds, the dwarf red-and-yellow sort indigenous to Mexico was growing in the royal gardens of Paris before the

sixteenth century was out. Not long afterward, both the giant and the miniature species made their way to England, where they were named for the places whence they'd come to the British Isles. John Gerard includes them in his *Herball* as "the great African double marigold" and "the great single French marigold."

Gerard, always interested in the medicinal uses of plants, is immoderately suspicious of the marigold. He objects to what he considers its "unpleasant smell" and refers to experiments made by the Flemish physician and botanist Rembertus Dodonaeus, who was born Rembert van Joenckema (back then, scientists—witness Carolus Linnaeus, once Carl von Linné—gave themselves latinized binomials, much like those of plants and animals). Gerard cites Dodonaeus's observations that he

> did see a boy whose whole lippes and mouth when he began to
> chew the floures did swell extremely; likewise he saith, we gave to
> a cat the floures with their cups, tempered with fresh cheese, she
> forthwith mightely swelled, and a little while after died: also mice
> that have eaten of the seed thereof have been found dead.

Gerard concludes that "these plants are most venomous and full of poison, and therefore not to be touched or smelled unto, much lesse used in meat or medicine." But the sheer beauty of marigolds must have disabused gardeners of such notions.

Gardens in North America received "African" and "French" marigolds from English and Dutch nurseries soon after the Revolutionary War, but by 1783, Mexico, too, was shipping its native plants north.

Marigolds possess not only beauty but also utility. Traditional wisdom has long led gardeners, without knowing why, to plant them as colorful companions for tomatoes. Scientific research has demonstrated that they secrete chemical compounds, known as thiophenes, that are toxic to many strains of bacteria, viruses, and fungi. More important, the roots of many varieties release a-terthienyl, a compound that kills both root-lesion and root-knot nematodes, those minuscule, parasitic worms that suck the juices out of tomato roots and stunt the plants. Another study has shown that marigold roots offer a home to bacteria that can decrease the population of root-lesion nematodes in the potato patch. The Burpee Company has developed a four-foot-tall single French marigold named 'Nema-Gone.' Another highly recommended variety is 'Toreador', which sports deep orange double flowers five inches across. With the exception of the tiny-flowered 'Gem' series, any other marigolds, short or tall, will do the nematode-repelling trick. I like the idea of height, however, for the tomato vines will not conceal the flowers, and the marigold stems may be tied to the tomato cages to keep them upright.

Marigolds' second trick (which strikes me as being not nearly so useful as the first) is that their gold petals—harvested, dried, powdered, and added to chicken feed—give a rich, orangey glow to egg yolks. But the diet of free-range chickens does not need this floral enhancement, for the yolks of their eggs are naturally bright orange from the weeds and insects that they consume. It is shoddy for poultry growers to use the color of innocent marigolds to bolster the color of eggs laid by chickens raised in brooder houses. Third, Gerard to the contrary, marigolds may be eaten without fear, especially the citrus-flavored *T. tenuifolia*, the "slender-leaved" species commonly known as 'Lemon Gem' and 'Tangerine Gem'. One book on edible flowers suggests putting them in salads, sprinkling them over broccoli, and adding them to the seasoned yolks of deviled eggs.

Marigolds are, bar none, the plants most willing to grow under almost any conditions. They love sun but tolerate shade, they sprout and thrive in hardscrabble soil, and they bloom right merrily from late spring to first frost.

ZINNIA (*ZINNIA ELEGANS, Z. HYBRIDA, AND Z. HAAGEANA*)

Tall, multipetaled zinnias of the "elegant" species share the wooden planter in the front yard with petite marigolds. A short "hybrid" variety with single petals grows beside the lima beans in back. Gold, white, light pink, dark pink, red, orange, yellow—the colors vibrate and sing. Some flowers are even variegated—yellow and rust, red tipped with white. And all that you need to do to start them is broadcast the seed. Willy-nilly, they sprout and grow. A major glory of the garden, they bloom all summer long.

Once upon a time, however, they were not glorious at all. The plant that the Spaniards found when they invaded Mexico in 1519 was an almost weedy perennial member of the Asteraceae, the Aster family. It produced prodigious numbers of rayed, daisy-like single flowers, but, unlike the New World's sunflowers and marigolds, its appearance was so drab that it was hardly noticed. The Aztecs did have a name for this common wildflower, a word that means "eyesore," which the Spaniards picked up and converted into *mal de ojos.* (The current Spanish word is simply *zinnia.*) The ordinary little flower might have stayed in Mexico but for the European interest in botany that exploded two hundred years later. With thousands of other genera, it was collected and taken to Europe. Linnaeus himself named it *Zinnia elegans,* a term coined to honor Johann Gottfried Zinn (1727–1759), a professor of medicine, who taught at the University of Göttingen in Germany. An ardent botanizer in the fashion of his day, Dr. Zinn had grown the plant from seeds sent to him by Germany's ambassador to Mexico. Though the Linnaean binomial refers to its elegance, the eighteenth-century plant still fitted into the eyesore category. Only in the 1880s did French horticulturalists start fiddling with the wildflower and in 1886 produced a truly colorful double zinnia. The ugly duckling seemed to have become a swan. The world paid attention.

The problem was that, like apple trees, the fancified zinnias did not breed true from seed. How on earth did we get today's profusion of reliable colors and sizes, from giants to dwarfs? The person who did the most to start zinnias on the way to their present popularity was the plant breeder Luther Burbank (1848–1926). Believing firmly in the Darwinian evolutionary model and in the inheritance of acquired genetic characteristics, he worked with an astonishing variety of flowers, fruit trees, vegetables, and grains to produce more than eight hundred new strains and varieties, with a special interest in plums and lilies. He was also responsible for developing the Shasta daisy. How he had time for zinnias is an unanswerable question, but toward the end of his life, he developed an eye-catching hybrid with petals like those of a dahlia. After his death, William Henderson, his gardener-in-chief, continued the master's work. In the early 1940s, Henderson's seed company was purchased by Burpee, the firm founded by William Atlee Burpee (1858–1915). Zinnias became the subject of many eager experiments for the next decade, but the seeds still failed to breed true. By the late 1950s, however, this trait had been successfully removed. Nowadays, if you plant the seeds of 'Burpeeana Giant' (*Z. elegans*), you can reliably expect cactus-flowered zinnias in many colors, while 'Old Mexico' (*Z. elegans*) will invariably produce double bicolors of yellow and dark rusty red and the tiny 'Profusion' zinnias (*Z. hybrida*) will always show their one-inch, single cherry-red, apricot-orange, or lemon-yellow flowers.

The zinnia possesses virtues that make it a highly desirable garden ornamental. Not least of them is that its weediness, now tamed but innate, enables it to adapt to a range of soil and climate conditions. Its odor discourages insect pests (although not slugs and snails, as I've learned to my sorrow; the answer here is to sprinkle the soil around zinnias with diatomaceous earth). But it loves sun and warmth and, in the Shenandoah Valley, thrives best in July and August. Perennial in places like Central America and Florida that are not struck by rigorous winters, the zinnia is an annual in most of North America. The ancestral wildflower still exists in Mexico, and, although I've seen an account stating that all zinnia species come from that country, they are also indigenous elsewhere, and some are native to southwestern states, including Texas and Oklahoma.

Elegant zinnias with large double flowers and single hybrid zinnias that grow only twelve inches tall—these always have room in my garden. They shall be joined by an alluring species with the trade name of 'Persian Carpet', *Z. haageana,* the species-name of which commemorates J. H. Haage (1826–1878), a German seed-grower. That Persia figures in the varietal name is geographically misleading, but it's meant to suggest the profusion of colors in these double and semi-double flowers: each blossom is a two-inch yellow-tipped pinwheel of red, rust, mahogany, purple, chocolate, and white. Wow!

✺ COSMOS (*C. BIPINNATUS* AND C. SULPHUREUS)

If ever a flowering plant thrived on neglect, the cosmos takes the prize. I have planted the seeds of *C. bipinnatus* in the back garden only once. They came in a gift packet accompanying my order of bean and squash seeds in the first year of my full-time return to Tomato Haven. The plant is an annual, but it may as well be perennial, for, since that first sowing, the delicate, ferny leaves have sprouted every spring. From then on the plants flourish, the stems proceed to grow to four or more feet in height, and the flowers, with petals ranging in color from light pink to deep rosy purple, bloom from mid-July until first frost. The plant seeds itself so liberally that, as long as there's a garden in back, it will contain cosmos.

Like zinnias and marigolds, cosmos are members of the Asteraceae, the Aster family. The genus is both native and introduced. The Southwest, Maine, Massachusetts, and Maryland boast wild populations of *C. parviflorus*, "small-flowered cosmos" or southwestern cosmos, while *C. caudatus*, "cosmos with a tail" or wild cosmos, is found in Florida, Puerto Rico, and the West Indies. The latter has also become naturalized in the South Pacific, where it is used in traditional medicine to make a postpartum decoction. But the two species of cosmos most widely grown in American gardens were introduced from Mexico: the white to purple-pink *C. bipinnatus*, "twice-feathered cosmos" or garden cosmos, and *C. sulphureus*, the common name of which translates the binomial—sulphur cosmos, which blooms yellow, orange, and red. "Twice-feathered" refers to the nature of the leaves, in which each leaflet sprouts leaflets of its own. As for cosmos, the word is a Greek term, which is usually translated as "world-order" and "universe." But my favorite definition comes from the philosopher Archimedes, who is cited in my Greek lexicon as using the word to mean "sphere whose center is the earth's center and radius the straight line joining earth and sun."

It took centuries for cosmos to make their way from the gardens of Mexico to this country. The Spanish conquistadores could not help noticing—and coveting—them. And in 1556, Spain established a policy to protect the vegetation of Mexico from exploitation by any other European country. A law was passed forbidding any foreign plant explorations and also any publication of data on the natural resources of Spanish territories in the New World. For two hundred years, cosmos and many other plants were kept secret from non-Spanish residents of the Old World. In the late 1700s, however, on his ascension to the Spanish throne, Charles III (1716–1788) decided to send a committee of naturalists and artists to explore and catalogue the flora of Spanish America. They embarked for Mexico in 1788 and proceeded to send a marvelous array of plants and seeds to Madrid's botanical garden, whence many were given away to aristocratic Spanish gardeners. One of them, Don Antonio Cavanilles, planted cosmos seeds and grew the Old World's first specimens. Unable to keep a good thing to himself, he gave seeds to the wife of the English ambassador—and just in time, for when Charles IV succeeded his father, he cancelled all botanical exploration in Greater Spain and forbade releasing the New World's plants into Old World gardens. But, in the late 1700s, the ambassador's wife had already taken the seeds back to England, where cosmos snuggled in and made itself thoroughly at home. The plant did not reach North America, however, until the 1890s, when the federal Plant Introduction Center was established. One task for the botanists at the center was searching for plants that would thrive in the deserts of the Southwest. They quickly found that cosmos fit the bill. In 1898, the plant came directly from Mexico into the U.S.

The problem with my tall and spindle-stemmed *C. bipinnatus* is that it takes only one hard rain to bend the plants clear to the ground. But being flattened doesn't faze them; the pink and purple flower-heads lift sunward, and the prostrate stems thrust down new roots. The trick to keeping them upright is to stake them or, as with tall marigolds, tie them to the tomato cages. *C. sulphureus* is on my seed-shopping list, for it offers varieties called 'Cosmic Yellow' and 'Cosmic Orange' that grow only a foot or so high.

Thinking of cosmos, I return to Archimedes and see its petals as the straight line joining earth and sun. This flower is truly a link between the mortal and the divine.

❧ BLANKET FLOWER (*GAILLARDIA ARISTATA*)

On both sides of the front garden, blanket flowers of the variety named 'Goblin' make a whirl of color—yellow, orange, red around a rusty disk—amid their ground-hugging but lush gray-green leaves. The plants are generous with flowers, each one presenting a dozen at a time. They are tender perennials, and it's always an iffy matter whether they'll make it back the following spring. For insurance, I grow more from seed at the same time that the cucumbers and peppers are sown in starter pots. Their blossoms, which come into fullness after the daylilies have ceased to flower, add bright fire to a patch of land that would otherwise be mostly green—herb-green, cucumber-green, broccoli- and cauliflower-green, hot- and sweet-pepper-green. Even the spent flowers are attractive, for they form fuzzy rust-brown balls. Nonetheless, to encourage bloom until first frost, I deadhead them every other day.

Like cosmos, blanket flowers belong to the Aster family (which certainly boasts many of the most desirable ornamentals). And blanket flowers of every species are native to North America, where they can still be found abundantly in the wild. The tender perennial in my garden is endemic to the West and southwestern Canada, and its common name reflects a notion that its colors and patterning resemble an Indian blanket. Its binomial, *G. aristata*, means "bearded Gaillardia," the beard being the soft bristles around the flower's receptacle, which is the part of the plant that bears its sexual organs.

As for the genus-name, it honors Gaillard de Marentoneau, an eighteenth-century French magistrate and botanist (though some sources say that he was not a botanist but rather a patron of botany). My *G. aristata* is a sprawling plant that grows no higher than a foot, but some cultivars have been bred to attain a height of four feet. An annual sort of single blanket flower, found in the wild in much of the U.S., is also grown in gardens. It's *G. pulchella*, "little-beauty Gaillardia," commonly known as firewheel. This species has been extensively fiddled with by the developers and is now available in a variety called 'Sundance Bicolor' that sports lushly double petals of dark red and deep yellow.

Like cosmos, blanket flowers are not finicky about growing in poor soil, and as plants originating in arid regions, they readily survive dry spells. Like cosmos, they self-sow. Last fall, I spotted the rosettes of two infant plants, one on each side of the front walk. Hurray!

⚜ BLACK-EYED SUSAN (*RUDBECKIA HIRTA*)

Black-eyed Susans are becoming a fixture in my garden. I had no intention at first of growing this species, but, as happens frequently, a gift packet accompanied an order of vegetable seeds—black-eyed Susan. It was a variety called 'Irish Eyes', which has a green disk instead of the usual brown or black in the center of each sunny yellow wheel of petals. This particular *Rudbeckia* is sometimes called a gloriosa daisy. I put the seeds in starter pots. They sprouted and grew big enough to transplant into a spot, newly denuded of grass, on the north side of the front yard. I put six seedlings into the ground.

During the next few days, they suffered a massive invasion by slugs and snails, and their number diminished until there was only one. It somehow withstood the attacking mollusks and grew so tall—to more than three feet—that it had to be staked. It put forth dozens of buds. They bloomed as promised: yellow spokes around a hub of pale green. But when the flowers were pollinated, the hub turned brown, and 'Irish Eyes' looked like any other Susan. But, as is the habit of *Rudbeckia*, a too-frequently short-lived perennial, 'Irish Eyes' lived and flowered for only three years. In the fourth spring, after waiting a decent interval, I planted a cayenne pepper in its place and placed nearby a truly black-eyed Susan, purchased at the farmers' market.

Black- and brown-eyed Susans, gloriosa daisies, cutleaf coneflowers—whatever the species of *Rudbeckia*, all are members of the Asteraceae, the Aster family, which includes another genus of plants—*Echinacea*—that are also aptly called coneflowers, like the pale purple coneflower (*E. pallida*) and the eastern purple coneflower (*E. purpurea*). (*Echinacea* comes from the Greek word *echinos*, "hedgehog," which characterizes the bristly scales on the cone.) The genus-name *Rudbeckia* has a long and honorable history. Linnaeus himself chose it to honor two of his professors, a father and his son, at the University of Uppsala in Sweden. The elder was Olaf Rudbeck, senior (1630–1702), who in the fashion of his day latinized his name to Olaus Rudbeckius. A polymath learned in science, engineering, and writing, he taught medicine at the university, served as its first instructor in botany, and founded its Botanical Gardens not long before his death. His son, Olaf Rudbeck, junior (1660–1740), a scientist and explorer, succeeded him as an instructor in botany and as curator of the university's celebrated Botanical Gardens. They would be delighted by the number of New World species that bear their name—not only *R. hirta* but also *R. californica*, *R. fulgida*, *R. grandiflora*, and a slew of others. The species names, respectively, mean "of California," "shining," and "large-flowered." It is *R. fulgida* from which the popular 'Goldsturm' strain was developed.

I miss 'Irish Eyes', which is no longer available through the company that sent it to me in the first place. But another company now offers a green-eyed variety called 'Prairie Sun', with flowers five inches across and bicolored petals of pale orange that lighten to golden yellow near the tips. Come spring, starter pots will be put in the cold frame.

✎ COREOPSIS (*C. GRANDIFLORA* AND *C. VERTICILLATA*)

Coreopsis is commonly known as tickseed because its seeds do indeed resemble bugs. The word "coreopsis" comes from the Greek and means "buglike." But when I look at the flowers in my yard, my mind focuses not on ticks but on whorls, pompoms, and petal-light of palest yellow and deep gold. Both the two-inch double *C. grandiflora*, "large-flowered coreopsis," and the daintier *C. verticillata*, a name that describes the single petals as "forming a ring around an axis," grow on the south side of my front yard. The latter, also known as thread-leaved tickseed, bears the varietal name 'Moonbeam', which would ring true only if moonbeams shone yellow. Amid the gaillardia, hosta, daylilies, oregano, and cayenne pepper plants, its flowers shine like bits of the sun. And the *C. grandiflora*, brought here from my North Carolina flower garden, brings thoughts of that flat-as-a-flounder coastal plain to this mountain-guarded valley in Virginia.

The coreopsis species are, of course, members of the Asteraceae, the Aster family. Native to North America, they are found growing in the wild in many states. Many are perennial, and even those that are annual in colder climates are perennial in subtropical regions. One of the latter is *C. tinctoria*, "coreopsis used in dyeing," which is an annual, biennial, or perennial depending on its location. Showing a rust-colored ring at the base of its yellow petals, it is the species selected by Florida as the state's wildflower.

As it happens, not just *C. tinctoria* but any species of coreopsis may be used in dyeing. I've made dye from the yellow flowers of *C. lanceolata*, "lance-leaved coreopsis," and with it turned snow-white wool to a golden orange. In fact, until I moved to Virginia in the late 1970s, I had a dyer's garden in Connecticut. It was inspired in the early '70s by a trip with my children to Sturbridge Village, the recreation of a colonial village near the Massachusetts town of the same name. There, amid broom-makers, blacksmiths, and householders, the women in one backyard had suspended a huge black iron kettle over a wood fire, and one was lifting a dripping hank of wool out of the pot. She hung it on a twiggy bush that bore other hanks in as many colors as Joseph's coat—blue, yellow, brown, rose, and green. Fascinated, I spent the rest of the morning there asking questions while my children (old enough to be civilized) finished their tour by themselves. Home again, I found books on dyeing and a shop that supplied wool suitable for hooking rugs, along with a rug frame and a punch needle. All that was necessary were the plants for making dyes and the mordants that would fix the colors in the wool. I dug up a small garden plot and set in marigolds (golden yellow), mullein (pale yellow), and goldenrod (brassy yellow) along with the coreopsis. Other dyes came from wild sources or the grocery store. The former included dandelions (pale yellow), barberries (greenish brown), and sumac berries (dark green and dark gray, depending on the mordant); the latter, tea (tea), sunflower seeds (pale gray-green), and onionskins (rich orange). It was as if earth herself were delivering up her truest tones. I designed and fashioned rugs, two of which I still possess. Knitting wool was also dyed and turned into sweaters with Icelandic patterns. My dye book, with samples and details of the dye-making, sits amid cookbooks on a kitchen shelf.

In many ways, my garden is a scrapbook, in which coreopsis commands several pages, for it connects me not just to the North Carolina days but to that busy spell of knitting and making punch-needle rugs in the 1970s. At the moment that I write, I'm planning a new coreopsis page: 'Sweet Dreams', *C. rosea*. With copywriter's hyperbole, the Burpee catalogue describes its colors this way: "blush white with a rosy-carmine ring around the center." "Blush white" does not, however, equate with white. It means "pale pink." I wonder what color dye this "rosy coreopsis" will produce.

≯ LANTANA (*L. CAMARA*)

The myriad little flowers—white, pale yellow, and pink—beckoned to me quietly at the farmers' market: lantana. The only plants that I'd intended to buy were sage and creeping rosemary, but head over heels, I succumbed. I'd grown lantana in North Carolina, a vigorous specimen with bold flowers of yellow, orange, and red that attracted airborne flotillas of butterflies all summer long. That's one of lantana's virtues—the long season of bloom. It has its vices, too, and I'll get to them shortly. But virtues and vices had nothing to do with my purchase of the young lantana in its six-inch pot. It was the plant's unassuming, innocent colors that beguiled me. Home again, before setting the rosemary and sage in the front-yard herb garden, I put the lantana on the south side of the backyard between the raised bed and the compost bin. There, in its accustomed fashion, it would have ample room to sprawl.

Lantana, sometimes called shrub verbena, belongs to the Verbenaceae, the Vervain family, which includes the teak tree of Asia (*Tectona grandis*); America's own beauty berry (*Callicarpa americana*) that bears a stunning electric-magenta fruit, and the red-flowered verbena (*Verbena* hybrid) that I like to set into the decorative pots on either side of my front steps. Its growth habit is indeed shrublike, and it can be used as a hedge plant. *Lantana* is the Latin word for "viburnum," while the species-name, which is a South American vernacular word for the plant, indicates its origin. But lantana has achieved worldwide distribution, thanks to the nursery trade, which has found profit in its come-hither colors. Not all the world is pleased, however, because the plant is a takeover artist that moves into any habitat that strikes its fancy, from natural forests to pastures to urban areas. Pacific islands, including Hawaii, and Pacific-rim nations like the Philippines, Australia, and Thailand have now been overrun to such an extent that lantana has been nominated in those parts as one of the top hundred of the world's most invasive plants. Once established, it's well-nigh unbudgeable. Drought does not perturb it, nor do frog-drowning rains. It can form thickets, which exclude species normally found in the understory. Nor does its mischief cease there, for its fruits are poisonous to cattle and other animals, and studies have shown that it secretes chemicals that are inimical to corn, squash, green beans, and tomatoes, all of them important crops. In other words, don't put lantana near your vegetables.

So, I've invited an invader into my yard—except that my plant-hardiness zone does not allow lantana to spread itself willy-nilly. Of all fifty states, only in Hawaii and Florida does it bloom year-round. In the Shenandoah Valley, the first hard frost will strike its leaves causing them to fall, and the stalks themselves are killed. The plant looks as if it can never again come alive. But it does—slowly. Well after the daylilies have burst into bloom, after the first scarlet flush of the climbing roses, new stalks of lantana will poke tentatively upward, as if tasting the air and the light. Within a week, they're a foot long, and the week after that, they leaf out. Then there shall be bloom from summer until the black days of November.

❧ SUNFLOWER (*HELIANTHUS ANNUUS*)

'Sunbright', 'Giant Sungold', 'Sunset', and 'Moonshadow'—these and many other names of sunflower cultivars attest to the colors of heaven. They invoke dawn and dusk, the whirl of the star-embraced moon, and the hot golden radiance of the sun. Still other names, like 'Lemonade', 'Dorado', 'Tangina', 'Strawberry Blonde', 'Claret', and 'Jade', describe the grand array of flower colors: yellow, gold, variegated yellow and red, dark red, and, yes, green. Yet other names focus on the plant's size—'Paul Bunyan' and 'Cyclops' for fifteen-footers, 'Elf' for a twelve-inch dwarf variety that's happy in a pot. Moreover, some sunflowers have been bred for double rays—they look just as fluffy as large chrysanthemums, while other varieties are advertised as providing superior seeds for roasting and popping into your mouth. No matter what their color, size, or use, the flowers grow on stout stems with large, wooly leaves.

Helianthus—the genus-name comes from Greek and translates, precisely, as "sunflower." The species-name, *annuus*, means what it looks like—"annual." Members of the Asteraceae, the Aster family, all *Helianthus* species are native to the Americas, and the Indians of North America cultivated them as food crops in fields long before the arrival of the first colonists. The Aztecs of Peru apparently venerated sunflowers, for they left carvings that show priestesses in the temples of the Sun wearing crowns of these flowers and carrying them. In the sixteenth century, the conquistadores found sunflowers wrought of gold in the temples. Of course, they took real seeds back home, and since then, *H. annuus* has been a wonder of the world. By 1580, the sunflower had become a common sight in Spanish gardens. And it quickly migrated along the trade routes to far-off lands like Afghanistan, India, Russia, and China.

Sunflowers also caught on quickly in England and France, which not only received seeds from Spain but also from their own explorers. John Gerard speaks admiringly of a sunflower that he grew from Spanish seed: "The Indian Sun or the golden floure of Peru is a plant of such stature and talnesse that in one Summer being sowne of a seed in Aprill, it hath risen up to the height of fourteene foot in my garden, where one floure was in weight three pounds and two ounces and crosse overthwart in the floure by measure sixteene inches broad." He also recognizes two distinct subspecies, *Flos solis major* ("greater sunflower) described above and *Flos solis minor* ("lesser sunflower"). The latter, he asserts, is dioecious, with male plants separate from those that are female. He's wrong here, but he may well be right when he tells us that the buds, oiled and eaten with butter, vinegar, and pepper are "exceedingly pleasant meat."

Today, it's the seeds that count. We can grow them, we can buy them, salted or not, in a store, and eat them like candy. They are far more nutritious than candy, though, for they contain truly significant amounts of phosphorus, iron, potassium, and thiamine. But growing seeds for snacking accounts for only 10 to 20 percent of the commercial market. Such food-grade seeds are called "confectionary." No one has come up with birdseed's percentage of the market, but several hundred thousand acres are devoted to growing it, and the acreage is bound to increase with the dramatic increase in the number of bird-aficionados. But oil is the raison d'être for most commercial production. Sunflower oil for cooking has several advantages over other vegetable oils: it is lower in saturated fats and is more stable, not needing hydrogenation to improve shelf life. But when it comes to sunflower oil, Americans were slow on the ball. Russians widely adopted its use in the 1800s. In America, however, its worth was not recognized until fifty years ago, and only in the last twenty-five years have oilseed plants begun to command significant acreage. And what do you do with what's left when the oil is expressed? Feed it to beef and dairy cattle as a good source of supplemental protein. Today more than three million acres are given to sunflower farming, 90 percent of it to the oilseed type.

To see a field of commercial sunflowers in full bloom, acre on acre reaching to the horizon, is to be drenched by their golden light. No wonder that Kansas has chosen it as the state flower. And, oh, what a wonder the flowers are! As with all the composite forms of the Aster family—coreopsis, cosmos, zinnias, black-eyed Susans, and the myriad others—each inflorescence comprises *two* types of flowers. The part that looks like petals consists of individual ray flowers, while the face of the flower head is a congeries of disk flowers, each of which forms a seed. In the early stages of growth sunflowers do track the sun but later stabilize themselves to face east before they bow their heads toward the earth. The bowing has been bred into them, for that lowered head makes it harder for birds to snack on the ripened seeds. This habit leads to a precept:

> *If a mature sunflower in your garden bends its seed-filled inflorescence downward, you know that it grew from a commercial, not an ornamental, cultivar.*

For the most part, the sunflowers that arise in my garden are a diverse, commercial, no-name bunch, planted by birds at the feeders. Most sprout in the vegetable patch, but no part of the yard is exempt from their presence. A tall, multiflowered specimen that bloomed and kept on blooming arose in the front yard beside the Japanese maple, which it dwarfed. For its appearance I can most likely thank a tufted titmouse or a Carolina chickadee. Some of the backyard plants have been gigantic with huge heads like that described by John Gerard; others are small, no taller than two feet with flowers that do not span my palm. Some produce only a single flower, but most bloom again and again, with new flowers appearing in the axils where leaves meet stem. Such diversity speaks to the fact that growers and packagers are interested in the practical aspects of sunflowers rather than in their ornamental qualities. I like the ornamentals, too, and started 'Velvet Queen' from seed in the cold frame. The seedlings were set amid the backyard broccoli, and when they flowered, the fiery color of their gold-tipped rust-colored rays contrasted delightfully with the cool silver-green of broccoli leaves. But, be they accidental or intentional, all sunflowers suffice for cutting and putting into vases so that they can spread their warm and sunny light indoors.

My garden's flowers form a peaceable kingdom. Not one is mightier than another, and no matter what their nationalities, their countries of origin, they do not disagree. I could preach a sermon on their finely tuned accord but shall forfend. It is enough to sow their seeds or set them in the earth, pat down the earth around their roots, weed them, and smile.

THE SECRETS OF
THE VEGETABLES

The vegetables are taking over
demolishing fences
obliterating property lines
let there be no more owners
and no more ownership
no more plats lots liens mortgages
let there be no property
even in the suburbs
let there be only the earth and the seeds
and the harvest thereof.

—*Constance Urdang,*
from "The Roots of Revolution
in the Vegetable Kingdom"

Butternut
SQUASH
BUSH BEANS

THE HEART OF MY GARDEN IS THE VEGETABLE PATCH. Despite Constance Urdang's wish that there be no more owners and ownership, the vegetables own me. I spend much of the spring and summer in their service. The pay, however, is not to be surpassed. It keeps me fed on the taste of summer all winter long.

GREEN BEANS

On June's arrival, the spring crops of broccoli and cauliflower, lettuce and radishes are done. When the summer solstice brings in the year's shortest night, it also summons ripening on ripening. The green beans are the first to say, Pick me. They were sown in mid-April; now their stems bend over under the weight of the pods. Those that are not eaten fresh will be blanched and frozen or canned in old blue Mason jars, the color of which deepens and intensifies the greenness of the beans.

Over the years, I've grown a variety of cultivars, all of the bush, rather than the climbing sort. Nor have all of them been green; yellow and dark purple sorts have also decked the bean patch with color. Some have been long and skinny, like the 'Blue Lake' variety, while others, like 'Kentucky Wonder' or the Italian types, are flat and wide. No matter their hue, all of them are *Phaseolus vulgaris*, the "common bean," and all originated in the New World, where they were grown for millennia before the Spanish conquistadores came clanking ashore in their armor. All are members of the order Fabales, which includes not only peas and beans but also peanuts, clover, mimosas, and kudzu. And all have developed a mutually beneficial symbiosis with nitrogen-fixing bacteria, which live amid their roots and convert aerial nitrogen into soluble nitrates; the plants then leave the nitrates in the soil, an event that increases its fertility.

Then, there's the Problem. Sixteenth-century botanist John Gerard has stated it well in his *Herball*: "The Beane is windie meate. And seeing the meate of Beans is windie, the Beans themselves if they be boyled whole and eaten are yet much more windie. If they be parched they lose their windiness, but they are harder of digestion." Beans, both fresh and dried, have ever been blamed, and rightly so, for causing flatulence. How so? Modern science has found the reasons. Dried beans contain two indigestible starches, stachyose and raffinose: the stomach growls, and the rump toots. Sugars are the villains in fresh beans; digestive enzymes in the upper intestine cannot break them down, but bacteria degrade them in the lower intestine and, so doing, produce gas. The Problem is remedied at my house by accompanying a meal containing any kind of bean with a heaping dish of applesauce.

There are a million ways to prepare snap green beans. One of the favorites in the South is to stew them for hours with salt pork. I relish them cooked at a low boil for five minutes, drained, and set aside, then seasoned with mushrooms that have been sautéed in lots of butter. And here's an easy recipe for a lunchtime salad:

❧ BEAN SALAD ❧

Ingredients
¾ pound fresh green beans, cut on the diagonal
1 small red onion, thinly sliced
¼ cup balsamic vinegar and olive oil dressing
salt and pepper to taste

- Parboil the beans for 3 or 4 minutes and drain. While they are still warm, put the beans in a large bowl and mix in the onion and salad dressing. Add salt and pepper to taste.
- Marinate the mixture in the refrigerator for 30 minutes. Then spoon into individual bowls.
Serves 4.

And serve the salad with fruit and crusty French bread.

❧ THE SUMMER GARDEN, FROM SOWING SEEDS TO TRIMMING

July comes blazing in. Its skies are blue and cloudless in the morning, dark and broody with thunderstorms in the late afternoon. Now the tomatoes swell on the vines and begin to blush, then redden. The peppers, both sweet and hot, turn red, too; it's stuffed pepper weather and salsa weather, as well. The stems of the carrots grow stout. The limas bloom. In the kitchen both pressure canner and blanching kettle find much work.

I could sink into this season, could let the heat relax my imagination until it thinks of nothing but processing the summer's bounty and sitting afterward on the front porch to read and sip iced tea. But gardens have a schedule of their own, and in July, it's time to think of putting in fall crops for wintertime feasts. Crops that love cooler days and nights, the cole crops like broccoli and cauliflower, need to be started by July's end for planting in mid-August. So, of course, I go looking for seeds—supermarket, hardware stores, garden centers, cooperative farm bureau—only to find that I'm completely out of luck. It seems that the distributors come sweeping in at the end of June to remove all unsold seeds. Luckily, the garden catalogues are still around; they don't get tossed until those for the new year come along. Hallelujah, I find exactly what I want—varieties of cauli and broc that are suited to this part of the world. And the woman who takes my order gives me a gift, the kind for which you do say, "Thanks." When she hears that I've looked futilely far and wide for a local source of seeds, she knocks a dollar off the shipping and handling charge. In this experience there dwells a precept:

When you buy seeds in the spring for summer bounty, make sure that you acquire some for fall crops, as well. The seeds won't lose their vigor in a short four or five months, and you'll have all you need without having to traipse fruitlessly all over tarnation or twiddle your thumbs while waiting for delivery by mail.

Starter pots saved from tomato and pepper seedlings are filled with potting soil and watered; the cole seeds, round as tiny beads, are placed in them gently; and the works set atop a water-filled tray with a plastic cover that's overlaid by a capillary mat. The seeds sprout in only three days.

Extra seeds for annual flowers should also be bought in the spring—dwarf and tall marigolds, zinnias of many petal-styles and colors, yellow California poppies (*Eschscholzia californica*)—to fill in the bare spots after the daylilies, their bloomtime over, are sheared to the ground. Sometimes, my own marigolds, those that began their flowering in May, provide some seed. The poppies tend to sow themselves and come up year after year.

As always, the act of planting is an act of hope. If all goes well—and there's never a guarantee that it will, there shall be seedlings within a matter of weeks. New marigolds should bloom before August is out, and, when October's cool blue brightness arrives, heads of cauliflower and broccoli should be ready for cutting. Imagination already savors them.

Nor is it just the daylilies that need to be cut back in July. Other perennials become bumptiously overgrown—oregano and savory—or pitifully scraggly, like the double coreopsis and the columbine. Cropped almost down to the earth, the columbine won't flower again but it does put forth masses of fresh new leaves. July and August, as well, are months for daily deadheading, too. When I go out to get the morning paper, it takes only a minute to pinch spent blooms from the blanket flowers and the red geranium with variegated leaves. Only a minute, yes, and when people tell me that they'd love to garden but don't because of all the time needed to keep things right, I answer with a precept:

If you set the work aside to be done on one designated day, the work seems endless. The solution is simple. Plant, till, harvest, shear, deadhead—no matter what the task, twenty minutes max every day is all it takes to keep a garden going, even a Total Garden like mine. Even someone with a nine-to-five job can manage twenty minutes. And if it should rain, well, gardens are patient. Take the day off.

There's another secret, too. Unlike so much that we do, gardens provide instant gratification once they're planted. Certainly, there's long-term planning involved—the garden dreaming throughout the winter, deciding exactly what to plant and where, then altering these notions time and again. All winter, the pages of catalogues rustle, and pencil sketches fill a steno pad. But when spring comes, the leaves of lilies and violets appear, barely breaking the ground at first but rapidly showing new growth. The newly set-in geraniums and tomatoes take root and stand tall. The seeds in the starter pots sprout. Minute by minute, it's almost possible to see them burgeon. When the summer solstice arrives, warm and sunny or hot and steamy, the fruits of labor begin to be there for the picking.

⊰⊱ COMPANION PLANTINGS

Before I introduce you to easy-to-grow vegetables other than my faithful green beans, it would be well to say a little about companion plantings—the friendly, protective pairings of flowers and vegetables or veggies with other veggies to help keep weeds, insects, fungi, and other pests in check. The happy relationship of marigolds and tomatoes has already been discussed (see pages 94–95). It's only one of many time-tested combinations.

Companion planting is nothing new in the annals of raising crops. Virgil mentions an old man who planted vegetables in rows along with white lilies, vervain, and poppies. The poet also advises using oak or elm trees, but not hazel, to support grapevines. But the practice of putting beneficial plants side by side was hardly confined to the Old World.

The Iroquois placed together the plants that they called the "Three Sisters"—corn, squash, and beans, and they told a story about how the three came to humankind. In the beginning, when Sky Woman looked down through a hole in the sky, she lost her balance and fell down into a boundless sea. When the animals saw her falling, they took earth from the seabed and spread it over the back of a huge turtle to make her a safe landing place. Turtle Island has since become North America. When she fell, Sky Woman was pregnant and, after landing on the earth-cushion, gave birth to a daughter. When the daughter was grown, she was impregnated by the West Wind (this happens in Virgil, too) but died while giving birth to twin sons. After Sky Woman buried her daughter in the earth of Turtle Island, three plants thrust up from the grave—corn, squash, and beans, food not only for the twins but for all humankind. Nor was it only the Iroquois who cultivated Three-Sister gardens. The practice was found among the Hidatsas of the Great Plains, the Zunis in present-day New Mexico and Arizona, and many other tribes.

The reasons for the worth of companion plantings are not entirely clear. Chemistry, for one, has not been much investigated. (Applied research applies only when pressing problems need solutions and there is money to be made.) But experience and observation over the centuries have produced some valid conclusions. Among the three sisters, for example, we find two types of win-win symbiosis. The cornstalks provide support for the pole beans, which in turn fix nitrogen in the soil, while the squash vines with their huge leaves act as a green mulch, preserving moisture and keeping down the germination of weed seeds. Thus, amid the threesome, we see spatial interactions and nitrogen fixation. Another reason for companion planting is trap cropping, which means setting in a plant that pests find more desirable than the one that you wish to raise. An example is using collards to lure the diamond-back moth away from cabbage; for a tip on trap cropping to keep Japanese beetles away from your roses, see page 171. Then, some companion plantings involve beneficial allelopathy—that is biochemical pest suppression, for which marigolds are famous when placed in the tomato patch. (The black walnut's competitor-killing juglone, a negative example of allelopathic chemical warfare, has already been mentioned on page 8, but suppression in this case aids only the black walnut, nothing else.) Yet another benefit that gardens receive from companion planting is the creation of habitats that attract and nurture beneficial insects and other arthropods, like ladybird beetles, mantids, and parasitic wasps.

The last are harmless to people but death to creatures like tomato hornworms. Such habitats bring a double benefit: they control pests and reduce or eliminate the use of pesticides. Finally, mixing and mingling different genera in a single garden, be it large or small, offers security; if weather, bad bugs, or failure to thrive does in one vegetable, others will survive and yield.

A cornucopia of books exists on companion plantings. They give details, for example, on using radishes to trap cabbage worms and planting daffodils to discourage mice. I offer here the table put together by the U.S., Department of Agriculture's National Center for Appropriate Technology.

COMPANION PLANTING CHART FOR HOME AND MARKET GARDENING
(compiled from traditional literature on companion planting)

CROP	COMPANIONS	INCOMPATIBLE
Asparagus	Tomato, Parsley, Basil	
Beans	Most Vegetables & Herbs	Onion, Garlic, Gladiolus
Beans, Bush	Irish Potatoes, Cucumber, Corn, Strawberry, Celery, Summer Savory	Onion
Beans, Pole	Corn, Summer Savory, Radish	Onion, Beets, Kohlrabi, Sunflower
Beets	Cabbage & Onion Families, Lettuce	Pole Beans
Cabbage Family	Aromatic Herbs, Celery, Beets, Onion Family, Chamomile, Spinach, Chard	Dill, Strawberries, Pole Beans, Tomato
Carrots	English Pea, Lettuce, Rosemary, Onion Family, Sage, Tomato	Dill
Celery	Onion & Cabbage Families, Tomato, Bush Beans, Nasturtium	

Corn	Irish Potato, Beans, English Pea, Pumpkin, Cucumber, Squash	Tomato
Cucumber	Beans, Corn, English Pea, Sunflowers, Radish	Irish Potato, Aromatic Herbs
Eggplant	Beans, Marigold	
Lettuce	Carrot, Radish, Strawberry, Cucumber	
Onion Family	Beets, Carrot, Lettuce, Cabbage Family, Summer Savory	Beans, English Pea
Parsley	Tomato, Asparagus	
Pea, English	Carrots, Radish, Turnip, Cucumber, Corn, Beans	Onion Family, Gladiolus, Irish Potato
Potato, Irish	Beans, Corn, Cabbage Family, Marigolds, Horseradish	Pumpkin, Squash, Tomato, Cucumber, Sunflower
Pumpkins	Corn, Marigold	Irish Potato
Radish	English Pea, Nasturtiums	Hyssop
Spinach	Strawberry, Faba Bean	
Squash	Nasturtium, Corn, Marigold	Irish Potato
Tomato	Onion Family, Nasturtium, Marigold, Asparagus, Carrot, Parsley, Cucumber	Irish Potato, Fennel, Cabbage Family
Turnip	English Pea	Irish Potato

Abiding by this list is somewhat like the game that I used to play when I walked home from elementary school. "Step on a crack, break your mother's back"—so went the jingle: I most assiduously avoided stepping on any of the cracks where one slab of sidewalk joined the next or on any of the fractures within a single slab. The theory was that even if I accomplished no good, neither was I causing harm. Why not keep dill out of the carrot bed but rather pair it with spinach and strawberries?

✤ CUCUMBERS

July: I not only deadhead the flowers when I fetch the morning paper, I also pick a cucumber or three.

Oh, the cucumbers! *Cucumis sativa*, the "cultivated cucumber," was probably first domesticated in northern India, where it still can be found in the wild. Christopher Columbus himself introduced the cucumber to the New World in 1493; with other Old World plants, like wheat, sugarcane, and citrus trees, it was part of the cargo of his second voyage. Like melons, pumpkins, and the summer and winter squashes, the cucumber is a member of the Cucurbitae, the Gourd family. Early on, around the time that Homer gathered together the *Iliad* and the *Odyssey*, cucumbers had spread both east and west, to China and to the Near East. They relish hot weather, and the vines can shoot out more than a foot overnight, their little tendrils grabbing any leaf or stem that they touch. They also attract striped cucumber beetles, tiny creatures, no more than a quarter-inch long with brown and yellow stripes from stem to stern, that carry a bacterial wilt, which makes the leaves droop and dry up. Out comes the shaker can of rotenone. That's a naturally occurring insecticide made from the roots of *Derris elliptica*, "elliptical leather-covering," also known as the poison vine, a climbing leguminous plant found from India to Indonesia. In the Far East, its toxin is sometimes used by fishermen to stun fish. Here, on the dry land of my front yard, it helps to halt the beetle's ravages. But even wilted vines can find new life, sending forth new leaves and tendrils, setting more fruits. Those produced by my little pickling-variety plants are spiny, though hardly dangerous, and the prickers come right off with washing. Some people experience a Cucumber Problem: eating them brings on gaseous bloating, flatulence, and burps. One solution is to avoid eating them altogether, but anyone who yearns for cucumber soup and salad and sandwiches may find relief in buying or growing one of the burpless varieties that have been bred so that they don't form seeds. Another remedy is to eat young cukes that have not yet set hardened seeds.

Not all of my cukes are destined for that salad pot in the fridge. Some will become crisp sweet pickle chips. Herewith, the recipe:

⋟ SWEET PICKLE CHIPS ⋞

Ingredients
14 large pickling-sized cucumbers
4 cups white vinegar
6 cups sugar
5 tablespoons mixed pickling spices
1 tablespoon salt

- Place the cucumbers in a large stockpot. Cover with boiling water. Let stand for 24 hours. Drain and repeat this process for 3 more days.
- On the fifth day, slice the cucumbers ¼-inch thick and return them to the stockpot. Bring the vinegar, sugar, pickling spices, and salt to a boil and pour the mixture over the cucumber slices. If the syrup doesn't cover the cucumbers, make enough so that it does. Let stand for 24 hours. Drain and reheat the syrup. Pour it over the slices again. Repeat for one more day.
- On the eighth day, drain the syrup and heat it to a boil. Add the cucumber slices and return to a boil. Pack in sterilized pint jars. Seal.

Makes 8 pints.

Yum! Serve at Thanksgiving and Christmas—if the pickles last that long.

July also brings moments of stasis. I wait for the tomatoes, large on the vine, to achieve full redness. I wait for the pods on the limas to form. I wait for the butternut squash to turn from a green-striped off-white to a ripe tan. Meanwhile, in the squash patch, the golden flowers, as big around as salad plates, bloom daily beneath the huge, fuzzy green leaves.

⊰ TOMATOES

August: Heat sits over the garden like a broody hen. But stasis is over. The tomatoes come in! The patch is not a large one—nine 'Better Boys' and three 'Yellow Pears', each accompanied by a protective marigold—but it will provide a winter's worth of plain canned tomatoes in Mason jars and stewed tomatoes in the freezer, as well as several months of tomatoes in sandwiches and salads. The disappearance of the last fresh tomato brings a sad resignation. Except for cherry and grape tomatoes, the grocery-store types, be they vine-ripened or not, completely lack the sun-sugared flavor of home-grown fruit. We aficionados must endure ten long months of tomato starvation before next year's crop comes in.

The 'Better Boys', chosen for their resistance to disease, are a determinate variety, a bushy hybrid that sets fruit, then stops yielding within two months. The little 'Yellow Pears', on indeterminate vines which bear fruit until they're done in by a black frost, are named for their shape, as are cherry and grape tomatoes. The scientific name of all tomatoes, no matter the variety, is *Lycopersicon esculentum*, "edible wolf-peach," perhaps because they seemed at one time to be a false peach, a peach in wolf's clothing. (Some botanists still call it *Lycopersicon lycopersicum*, the genus-name Greek and the species-name Latin, a combination that effectively redoubles the wolfishness.) The common name comes from *tomatl*, an Aztec word picked up by Spanish missionaries and explorers. For tomatoes originated in the New World, and the ancestor from which all others were developed bore fruits that looked like clusters of red currants. The fruit is technically a berry. European botanists recognized the plant as a member of the Solanaceae, the Nightshade family, and that gave some of them considerable pause about its suitability for eating, for it was well known that some of the Nightshades, like mandrake and jimsonweed, are truly poisonous. In the 1633 edition of his *Herball*, English botanist John Gerard, shrugging off suspicion, grew a red variety in his own garden and was familiar with a yellow sort but claimed that they offer little nourishment to the body. He also ascribes to the whole plant a "ranke and stinking savour." In a pre-Linnaean age, he called them Apples of Love and went on further to say:

> The Apple of Love is called in Latine *Pomum Aureum, Poma Amoris,* and *Lycopersicum*: In English, Apples of Love and Golden Apples: in French *Pommes d'amour.* Howbeit there be other golden Apples whereof the Poets do fable, growing in the Gardens of the daughters of *Hesperus,* which a dragon was appointed to keepe, who, as they fable, was killed by *Hercules.*

Although Gerard clearly distinguishes between the edible Golden Apples and those fabled by the poets, I am caught in a moment of speculation: The Golden Apples of the Hesperides belonged to Hera, the jealous wife of Zeus, who did not want to share their radiant sweetness with anyone else. But suppose, oh just suppose that those fabulous apples were truly *yellow* tomatoes! The thought drives me to the kitchen where I pop a little yellow pear into my mouth. Divine!

It's the red tomatoes, though, that command much time and attention. I try to grow and process enough to see me through until the new season arrives. Canned tomatoes are destined for lasagna and the heirloom chutney that my grandmother called "Hellfire" because it'll raise blisters on food, not to mention the roof of your mouth. The stewed tomatoes are delicious by themselves or as the main ingredient of spaghetti sauce. Sweet peppers and basil grown in my garden add to their savor. To measure the quantity of tomatoes, I use the flat cardboard trays that hold four six-packs of beer or those that are used by garden centers or farmers' markets for customers to tote away plants and veggies. Herewith, the recipe:

⁑ STEWED TOMATOES ⁂

Ingredients
1 tray of tomatoes

1 medium onion, diced
1 sweet green pepper, diced
1 teaspoon dried basil (or 1 tablespoon fresh)
½ teaspoon sugar

- Scald and peel the tomatoes. Cut them into small chunks and place them into a 5-quart soup pot. Add the onion, pepper, basil, and sugar. Bring to a boil, then reduce heat, and simmer for 2½ hours.
- Ladle the mixture into pint bags or boxes. Let cool and then freeze.

NOTE: If some juice is left over, store it for later use in making Spanish rice or soup.

Makes 4 to 5 pints.

My friend Jeffery Beam, poet, manic gardener, and botanical librarian, has called upon his muse Dame Kind, doyenne of the natural world, and given me this brand-new poem:

TOMATO

Nightshades
on dry river banks
in warm mists

Xitomatl, tomate
Mala aurea, pomodoro
pomme d'amour
Love apple so long feared

So fully fat in juice
highly marriageable

Trailing the ground

True, all of it. The ancestral nightshade is imagined. The names are charted, from Aztec to sixteenth-century English. The vines do trail the ground, unless they're staked or caged; where the stems touch earth, new roots sprout. And the fruit is indeed marriageable, melding with soups, stews, and sauces. Thanks to canning and freezing, there is no doubt that tomatoes themselves make good poetry that may be revisited time and again.

⚜ CAULIFLOWER AND BROCCOLI

August's garden commandments continue. The patch of earth in the back garden, where July's green beans grew, is tilled for the fall crops of cauliflower and broccoli, as is the cucumber patch in front; the seeds for the plants have been started in small pots on the front porch, and the seedlings will be big enough to plant at the end of the month. I grew spring crops of both, too, planted in late March, harvested a month before the summer solstice. They produced nicely but not nearly enough to keep me going through the winter. Raw or cooked, both are delicious. Just thinking of them makes my mouth water. As for the garden, it, too, benefits, for the heavy shade cast on the earth below by the great gray-green leaves of broccoli and cauliflower keeps the usually brash weeds from popping up.

Chockful of potassium, vitamin C, fiber, antioxidants, and other valuable nutrients, both are cole crops, belonging to the Brassicaceae, the Mustard family, as do cabbage, brussels sprouts, kale, kohlrabi, and collards. "Cole," a catch-all term for those named veggies, comes from the medieval English word *colewort*, which means "cabbage plant." Indeed, the ancestor of them all is cabbage, which is blessed with a notably high quotient for genetic variation. In its earliest incarnation it was a loose-leafed, wild plant; the truly compact form grown today was not developed until the twentieth century. All of the coles share a single scientific name, *Brassica oleracea*, which translates as "garden cabbage." Each kind is differentiated from the others by a tacked-on group name. *Botrytis*, "grapelike," distinguishes cauliflower from broccoli, which is identified as *italica*, "from Italy." Broccoli truly originated in the Middle East but arrived in Italy in ancient times; the Romans cultivated it. The plant reached England by way of Italy long centuries later in 1720.

Cauliflower was found in English gardens long before then. The 1633 edition of John Gerard's *Herball* describes the plant (the name of which, in an age of uncertain orthography, he spells "Cole-Florie," "Cole-Flore," "Cole-florey," and "Colieflore" all in the space of three pages): it

> hath many large leaves sleightly indented about the edges, of a whitish greene colour, narrower and sharper pointed than Cabbage: in the middest of which leaves riseth up a great white head of hard floures closely thrust together.

He also reports that if cauliflower is eaten raw before consuming meat, it will "preserve a man from drunkennesse: the reason is yeelded, for that there is a natural enmity betweene it and the vine, which is such, as if it grow neere unto it, forthwith the vine perisheth and withereth away." According to Gerard, the juices of coleworts also act as a remedy against "the bitings of venomous beasts." Both cauliflower and broccoli came to North America with the colonists; both were regularly grown in Thomas Jefferson's gardens at Monticello near Charlottesville, Virginia.

How on earth did cabbage, loose or tight, beget broccoli with its silvery leaves and dark green heads of tightly clustered flower buds? How did it come to produce cauliflower with nearly ball-like white curd, composed of thickened, modified flower structures? Old-fashioned genetic modification, that's how. New-fashioned GM inserts genetic material into a cell, while variations on the cole theme (and uncountable other plants) were brought into being by careful observation and highly selective breeding. Both the cauliflower and broccoli forms of *Brassica oleracea* arose when farmers and other plantsmen concentrated on cabbage's flower buds rather than the leaves and developed plants that put forth the most prominent, well-packed, and tasty buds. Herewith, tasty ways to serve them:

⇘ BROCCOLI CASSEROLE ⇙

Ingredients
1 head broccoli, cooked and cut into bite-sized pieces
2 cups prepared stuffing
1 small onion, finely diced
water, enough to moisten the stuffing
butter
1 cup cheddar cheese, shredded

- Lightly grease a 9-inch-by-9-inch baking dish. Cover the bottom with the broccoli. Place slim pats of butter atop the broccoli.
- Mix the stuffing and onion with enough water to moisten it. Layer the stuffing mixture over the broccoli. Cover everything with cheese.
- Bake at 350° Fahrenheit for 15 minutes, or until the cheese is melted and bubbly.

Serves 4 modest appetites.

I often use leftover broccoli for this dish and adjust the other ingredients proportionately. Cauliflower is amenable to the same treatment, but in my kitchen, it's often featured in a soup:

⇘ SPICY CAULIFLOWER AND POTATO SOUP ⇙

Ingredients
1 tablespoon olive oil
1 medium onion, chopped
3 large cloves garlic, chopped
2 medium red potatoes, unpeeled

1 large head fresh cauliflower
1 4½-ounce can mild green chiles
1 fresh hot red pepper (jalapeño, cayenne, your choice),
    seeded and minced
salt and pepper to taste
6 cups chicken broth
1 cup sharp cheddar cheese, grated

- Heat the oil in a large soup pot. Add the onion and
  sauté, stirring occasionally, until translucent, about 5
  minutes. Add the garlic.
- Meanwhile, cut the potatoes into 1-inch cubes. Add them
  to the pot. Cook for 10 minutes, stirring occasionally.
- Add the cauliflower, chiles, hot red pepper, salt, and pepper. Stir in the chicken broth. Bring to a boil. Reduce the
  heat, cover, and simmer for 15 minutes, until the potatoes and cauliflower are tender.
- Remove from the heat. Working in batches, blend until
  smooth. Return the puree to the pot. Bring to a boil,
  adding water if necessary. When the soup is hot, ladle it
  into bowls and garnish with the cheddar cheese.
Serves 6.

Mid-August twelve cauliflower seedlings and twelve of broccoli
are set into the sweet brown earth. I look at them and think of pearls
and jade. I wait for casseroles and soup.

⚘ BUTTERNUT SQUASH

Mid-August is also the time for picking the butternuts, the golden
member of the Three Sisters, which were planted in mid-May, and
storing them temporarily on the back porch in cardboard boxes.

Members of the Cucurbitae, the Gourd family, the butternuts
and other winter squashes, including pumpkins, are indigenous
to the Americas, as are many of their close relatives, the gourds,

summer squashes, and melons (though some of the last are indeed native to the Old World). Most winter squashes are designated as *Cucurbita maxima*, the "greatest gourd," but the scientific name of butternuts is *C. moschata*, the "musky gourd." Squashes were domesticated in the New World some nine millennia before the first Europeans arrived. Almost as soon as the explorers did get here in the sixteenth century, they transported these delicious edibles across the Atlantic. Unlike the summer squashes, which must be picked and eaten before their seeds harden, the winter varieties are best when their seeds are set. And, oh, they are tasty, unlike their summer cousins, which must be gussied up with salt, pepper, butter, onions, and cheese before they have any flavor. The winter squashes are also more packed with nutrients—protein, fat, and vitamin A— than the summer sort.

Butternut with its rich golden-orange flesh is my favorite winter squash, bar none.

My harvest does not stay long in temporary storage on the back porch. It's variously given to neighbors and friends, and I take some, as well, to my exercise class at the Y. But there's a rule of thumb, here, too: don't run short. So, several butternuts are saved for baking with brown sugar and butter or with a slice of bacon. Others are steamed, their pulp put through a Foley Food Mill and stashed in pint and pint-and-a-half freezer boxes to assure a winter's worth of mashed butternut, butternut soup, butternut bread, butternut cookies, and butternut pie. For the last, I prefer butternut squash to its close relative the pumpkin, for many pumpkin cultivars are chockful of stringy filaments and yield their pulp reluctantly. The only ways around that problem are to buy cans of pumpkin or fresh, stringless varieties developed for pie-making or to forget pumpkin altogether. Mashed butternut may be used instead in any pumpkin recipe.

But many recipes featuring butternut squash instruct that the squash be halved, peeled, seeded, cut into small cubes, cooked, and pureed. What a time-consuming nuisance! I go to my freezer and haul out a box of squash that's already mashed. For Hallowe'en (and any other day), cake-like butternut cookies make a handy-dandy treat:

✤ BUTTERNUT-RASIN COOKIES ✤

Ingredients
2½ cups flour
1½ teaspoons baking soda
½ teaspoon salt
1½ teaspoons cinnamon
½ teaspoon nutmeg
2 eggs, lightly beaten
1 cup brown sugar
½ cup granulated sugar
½ cup butter (or shortening)
1 cup mashed butternut
1 teaspoon vanilla
½ cup milk
1 cup raisins
1 cup chopped walnuts (optional)

- Preheat the oven to 350° Fahrenheit.
- Stir together flour, baking soda, salt, cinnamon, and nutmeg in one bowl. In another bowl, beat the eggs and add brown sugar, granulated sugar, shortening, butternut, vanilla, and milk. Mix. Add flour mixture to sugar mixture and blend well. Add raisins and nuts.
- Drop by spoonfuls onto a greased baking sheet. Bake for 15 to 18 minutes, till golden brown.

Makes 60 cookies. The recipe is easily halved.

✤ CARROTS

Along with cookies, pots of soup, pickles, and the few spare butternuts, jars of carrot marmalade go into the hands of others. I've planted 'Nantes Half Long' and 'Touchon' carrots, the former as fat at the end as at the top, the latter tapering to a point. Both are cultivars that grow to a length of six or seven inches and so fit well into the ten-inch raised bed. I sprinkled a packet of each on the bed's almost black soil. Then, scratching away for who knows what, squirrels distributed the seed so nicely that there was no need to thin the sprouts.

Like all vegetables, carrots have a venerable history. They are members of the Umbelliferae or Carrot family, which includes parsley. The scientific name, *Daucus carota*, means "Carrot carrot," and the reason for that redundancy is that the repetition occurs in two languages: *Daucus* is Greek and *carota*, Latin. The very same binomial is given to Queen Anne's lace, ubiquitous on summer roadsides and in fields, and it deserves this designation, for it is our domestic carrot's Eurasian ancestor. But try eating the root of Queen Anne's lace—it's decidedly bitter. Must have been a soul on the verge of starvation who first took a bite of such unappetizing stuff. The carrot as we know it comes to us from two sources: southern Europe, where a white form was first cultivated, and central Asia with both a yellow and a violet form. This root vegetable arrived in Spain with the Moors but did not make its way to northwestern Europe until the thirteenth century. And it was the Spanish who first brought the carrot to the New World, to Hispaniola and other Caribbean islands, around 1520 as one of the crops, along with garlic, eggplants, and turnips, that they'd favored at home. Carrots, however, did not like the sultry subtropical weather. But when Hernán Cortés invaded Mexico, he recognized the similarity of its geography and climate to those of Spain and ordered direct shipments to Mexico of the vegetables with which he was familiar. But the carrot of the conquistadores wasn't orange. The color that invariably springs to mind these days when we think of carrot was developed in Holland in the late 1600s as a cross between the yellow and violet sorts. The sixteenth-century English botanist John Gerard ascribed marvelous powers to the carrot, writing that it "serveth love matters" and "containeth in it a certain force to procure lust." Might it be that Carrot, that tumescent root, would be effective as an inexpensive stand-in for Viagra?

I once raised 'Sweet Sunshine', a yellow variety of carrot. The seeds were duly planted in the rich soil of the raised bed. And when the stems had gained a stoutness indicating that carrots lay below, I pulled one. Orange! Not one hint of yellow, not outside nor in! I learned that by eating it almost as soon as I brought it into the kitchen. But before I ate, I photographed the carrot beside the seed-packet clearly imprinted 'Sweet Sunshine' and sent the photo, with a query, to Burpee. In due course, a postcard arrived: "We don't know why your carrots are orange." So, all I can do is guess, and my guess is that the rich soil turned a carrot that should have been lemony yellow into Bugs Bunny orange. The existence of an empty seed packet that could be used in the photograph leads to a precept:

Keep empty seed packets and mark each one with the date on which you sowed the contents. Packets contain much information about planting, germination times, and days until harvest. And you never know ahead of time when you might need to take a packet's photograph, along with the vegetable or flower it produced.

By mid-August, the orange roots in the raised bed have plumped out. The first harvest, including its ferny leaves, fills two five-gallon buckets. I have over half a bucketful after the leaves and spindly ends have been put into the compost bin, and there are yet more carrots to be picked—carrots for eating fresh like candy, carrots cut and blanched for the freezer and future stews, carrots for carrot cake, and carrots for marmalade. Herewith, another recipe:

CARROT MARMALADE

Ingredients
4 medium lemons
2 medium oranges
4 medium carrots, shredded

1½ cups water
6 cups sugar
6 ounces liquid fruit pectin

- Grate or slice off the peels of the lemons and oranges. If they're sliced off, cut them into very thin strips. Remove the white parts and thinly slice the fruit.
- Add the carrots and the water to the fruit and peels. Bring to a boil. Then reduce the heat and simmer for 10 minutes.
- Add sugar and bring to a hard boil. Boil for 2 minutes.
- Stir in the pectin and boil for 2 more minutes, stirring often.
- Ladle into sterilized jars and seal.

Makes 7½ to 8 half-pints.

The carrots deepen the marmalade's naturally orange color. The grating and the removal of fruit from the membranes—making this treat takes time. But, oh, the work is sweetly worthwhile. And often, honoring the principle of Don't Run Short, I find myself cooking up at least two batches.

⇝ PEPPERS, SWEET AND HOT

September: The days and the nights begin to cool, but the peppers, both hot and sweet, catch fire. Five varieties, one sweet and four with varying ranges of heat, grow in the front and back gardens. The sweet peppers are found in front, two of them in the decorative planters that rest on either side of the front porch steps, one in the ground just under the climbing 'Blaze' roses. They're a variety known as 'The Godfather', and they don't resemble bell peppers at all. Rather, the pods are six or seven inches long, wide at the stem end and tapering to a rounded point at the tip. Some are straight, some gently curved. I was attracted to them because of their hornlike shape and because of the catalogue's promise that they would turn beautifully red. Well, green bell peppers are also destined to turn red at maturity, but I'd never succeeded in producing one that was more than half red before it began to spoil. Not so with the 'Godfather'. The sign of turning is that its green becomes slightly brown. Then, after the peppers have become totally scarlet, they stay firm. Herewith, a precept:

Experiment with different varieties. Pleasant surprises are bound to occur.

The front yard also contains the cowhorn cayenne, which produces extremely long, plump, curved berries—yes, as for tomatoes, that's the proper botanical word for the kind of fruit produced by peppers (though pod will also do), and the cowhorn berries start turning red at the tip, with the blush working gradually up to the stem. And that cayenne is accompanied by two specimens of another cayenne cultivar, 'Joe's Long Cayenne', skinnier and straighter than the cowhorn type but just as long. This particular hot pepper, which I started from seeds in the cold frame, is said to be descended from seeds that came from Calabria, the region comprising the toe of Italy's boot. In the backyard, jalapeños flourish, along with one Anaheim and two tabasco plants. The name jalapeño derives from Xalapa, a city in Veracruz, Mexico, and cayenne, perhaps from the capital city in French Guiana but more likely from *cayan*, the word used for the plant by the Tupi Indians of that region. The generally mild Anaheim was developed in the California city of that name as a pepper so uniform in size that it can easily be canned. The berries are slender and supposed not to be nearly so long as either of the cayenne types growing in my yard, but mine have developed into giants as big as the 'Godfathers'.

As for the tabascos, when I bought them at a local garden center, I had no idea what their fruit might look like. Behold, on plants fully five feet high, the tiny peppers do not hang pendulous below the leaves but rather rise vertically like pale yellow candles an inch high and no more than a quarter-inch around at their widest end. The small white flowers washed with green also hold their heads aloft, looking toward the sun. These peppers shall turn orange, then bright red.

As usual, I'm curious. Whence these peppers? What is their lore? As it happens, all the world's peppers, no matter that they're hot or sweet, originated in Central and South America, where some may still be found in the wild today. The seeds have been found as fossils 9,000 years old, and archaeological evidence indicates that Indians had domesticated them as early as 4,000 B.C. The wide dispersal of various varieties throughout the inhabited world began when they were brought to Spain in 1493. And all peppers belong to the Solanaceae, the Nightshade family, as do tomatoes, eggplant, potatoes, and tobacco. Most of them, including my garden's 'Godfathers', jalapeños, cayennes, and lone Anaheim are *Capsicum annuum*, "the biter that grows annually." The tabasco variety, however, is designated as *C. frutescens*, "the shrublike biter," for its height. The varietal name was given to it in pre-Columbian times by the Olmecs who lived in the humid lowlands of what are now Veracruz and Tabasco states; the word means "damp earth." This chile is the sizzling ingredient of the famous sauce made after three years of fermentation in barrels by the McIlhenny Company in New Iberia, Louisiana. The common name of the hellishly hot habañero, *C. chinense*, "the Chinese biter" (though it has nothing to do with China), means "of Havana" and indicates an origin in the Caribbean, if not in Cuba itself. I am chastened to learn that any pepper pod capable of scorching the tongue and palate is properly called a chile, from *chilli*, the name used originally by Mexico's Náhuatl Indians. The proprietor of a Web-based encyclopedia of spices writes in a sternly chiding tone that "chiles are often referred to as *peppers* in English, which is of course a never-ending source of culinary fatal misunderstandings."

The use of chiles may also lead to other close-to-fatal consequences. John Gerard, who calls the pepper berries "cods," has this to say about the plant that he calls "Ginnie pepper" to distinguish it from the black pepper (*Piper nigrum*) put into shakers and grinders:

> Ginnie pepper hath the taste of pepper, but not the power or virtue, notwithstanding in Spaine and sundrie parts of the Indies they do use it to dresse their meate therewith, as we doe with Calcute [black] pepper: but it hath in it a malicious qualitie, whereby it is an enemie to the liver and other of the entrails. *Avicen* writeth that it killeth dogs.

Beware of the pepper from Guiana, though Gerard admits that it has some benefits, such as warming the stomach and helping with the digestion of meat. But Avicen is the Iranian physician Avicenna, who died in 1037 and could not possibly have known about an American berry that did not arrive in his part of the world until more than four hundred and fifty years later. Avicen was surely referring to "Calcute pepper."

Once upon a time, in the Carolina gardening days, I had an encounter with the malicious quality of chiles. Four habañero plants, acquired from a garden center, were placed amid coreopsis and zinnias in a small raised bed. And they flourished. Knobby yellowish pods about the size of a walnut formed and in the ripeness of time turned deep orange. With salsa and seasoning for soups aforethought, I made two harvests. With the first, the glowing little pods were cut in half, the stems and seeds removed, and the halves placed in a dehydrator. It took four days to dry them thoroughly, for the flesh holds considerable water. But when at last they were properly dessicated, they were stored in heavy-duty plastic bags and stashed in the freezer. The second harvest resulted in a hot sauce consisting of finely ground pods, vinegar, and salt. And with the making of that hot sauce, I learned a lesson:

When handling chiles, be they mildly hot or savagely so, always protect your hands. Wear the inexpensive

*rubber gloves that may be bought at any drugstore
and discarded after use.*

I did wear gloves for processing the habañeros that were dried. For the hot sauce, I did not. *O me miserum*! Unhappy me! Why I failed to use common sense, I do not know. I do know that the heat could not be washed off my hands, which burned for a full twelve hours after I'd put the last habañero in the sauce pot. But *burn* is too modest a word. My palms felt as if they were being licked by live flames. Nor was it possible to touch my mouth, nose, or eyes.

Pleasure and pain—both are incarnate in chiles. And my friend Jeffery Beam sends me a chile poem. The quotation comes from the Franciscan friar Bernardino de Sahagún (c. 1500–1590), who spent much of his life in Mexico as a missionary and anthropologist studying the Aztec language and culture. He also produced twelve volumes on these subjects. His words say much about Aztec foods and imply that a liberal slathering of chiles makes anything palatable.

BRING ME A PLATE

Setting the mouth's fire
that glands flow freely
leaving the mouth moist cleanly

"Frog with green chillis
Newt with yellow chillis
Tadpoles with small chillis
Maguey grubs with a sauce of small chillis
Lobster with red chilli"

Pleasure and pain
Capsicum

The villains are capsaicin and capsaicinoids, volatile compounds that retain their strength in the chile for a long time. In the time of the conquistadores, Indians burned chiles to repulse the invaders with the vapors of capsaicin. The compounds reside not in the flesh but in the placental membrane to which the seeds are attached. The heat of a chile is measured in Scoville Heat Units (SHU), using a taste test developed by Wilbur Scoville (1865–1942) in 1912. The way in which the test works is this: a human taster judges the heat of a specimen from hot to hotter to hottest; then sugar is given to the taster until heat no longer affects the mouth. The more sugar given, the higher the SHU of that variety. Today high performance liquid chromatography is used to measure capsaicin levels, which are still described, however, in terms of SHU. The chiles in my yard range from heat that's barely perceptible to heat that's respectably (not agonizingly) hot: Anaheim, 1,000–1,400 SHU; jalapeño, 3,500–4,500; cayenne, 30,000–35,000; and tabasco, 30,000–50,000. Those habañeros that almost did me in are hotter by far at an SHU quotient of 200,000–300,000. But even with the gentle Anaheims, I wear gloves.

One contemporary writer, Richard Schweid, offers enthusiastic support for popping hot chiles into the mouth whole, chomping on them, and washing them down with cold beer. That's "a habit well worth acquiring," he writes. "It stimulates digestion, clears the sinuses, and seems to be of benefit to the respiratory system. Equally important, *Capsicum* is a psychotropic plant. It heightens the awareness of a given moment by disrupting normal thought patterns and attention spans. It is hard to read the newspaper or dwell on one's usual cares while eating hot peppers." It's not for nothing that Italians call hot peppers *diavoletti*, "little devils."

For me, a little psychotropism goes a long way. But what shall I do with my cornucopious abundance of chiles? One likely product is a ristra, a handstrung rope of dried chiles that may be hung decoratively in the kitchen and plucked as needed. (Imagination sees a wreath composed of Anaheims and evergreen boughs placed on the front door at Christmas.) Another is pickled jalapeños, the ingredient sine qua non of a tomato-lettuce-red onion-black olive submarine sandwich. Yet another might be a homemade Tabasco sauce that has the consistency of a relish rather than a liquid. But if you try to find a recipe for manufacturing your own Tabasco sauce, any search engine will send you forthwith to recipes that merely use the McIlhenny Company's famous bottled fire. Instructions on making anything at all from homegrown tabascos seem completely absent. But a little thought, along with decades of kitchen experience, came up with a perfectly acceptable recipe (don't forget to put on your gloves). Warning: it clears the sinuses and makes you cough.

❧ HELLISH RELISH ☙

Ingredients
1½ cups red ripe tabasco chiles, finely chopped
2 cloves garlic, pressed
⅓ cup white vinegar
1 tablespoon fresh lime juice
slight sprinkle of salt
slight sprinkle of sugar

- Remove the seeds from the chiles and chop them in a food processor.
- Mix together all the ingredients in a stainless saucepan. Bring to a boil, reduce heat, and simmer for 5 minutes.
- Seal in a sterilized jar. Use judiciously to season soups, hamburgers, and other foods that need a dollop of zing.
Makes ½ pint. Stores well in the refrigerator after being opened.

Sometimes, though, I don't bother with a sterilized jar but simply spoon the relish into a glass storage jar that's put right away into the refrigerator. This relish has been used instead of supermarket ground red pepper to add the necessary heat to my grandmother's heirloom Hellfire chutney.

Oh, the chiles! A ristra of Anaheims hanging from a cup hook, jalapeños pickled in pint jars, dried and crushed cayennes in glass spice bottles, tabascos in the fridge—the possibilities for psychotropic moments seem infinite.

⚜ SOLARIZATION

September: The butternuts are in—four dozen of them. A few small tomatoes still hang on the determinate vines; they'll be converted into pickles. The yellow pear indeterminates, however, are still producing merrily and offering a taste of waning summer. So are both the sweet peppers and the hot ones. But the weeds are taking over, fall is in the air, the nights grow cooler. The time has come to put the garden to bed, to till it once more with the mini-tiller, and to anchor in the now empty squash patch the big cardboard boxes that I've broken down so that they lie flat. That way, fall weeds will be discouraged and spring tilling made easier without all those roots to go through. And the patch in which the 'Better Boy' tomatoes grew will be treated by solarization. This year wilt, a fungal problem, affected a quarter of the plants. Because tomatoes are rotated for three successive years, they'll not be planted in the same place next year. Meanwhile, not only wilt but other fungi, wintering grubs, and weed seeds can be done in by laying sheets of clear (not black) plastic over the tilled ground and pinning them down. It's a method seen often along highways on the medians and roadsides where wildflowers will be planted later. Sun shines on the plastic and cooks the dickens out of anything below.

I begin to think of my own upcoming hibernation, of my wintertime separation from the earth. But it's only the physical earth that will be put aside. For every gardener, even in the depths of cold weather, imagination sees the earth as green and abounding in flowers and fruits. And my shelves are laden with jars of tomatoes and pickles, the freezer with bags and boxes of veggies, enough to see me through until next year's harvest. Thanksgiving and Christmas dinners, not to mention everyday meals with family and friends, will be filled with the flavors of earth, air, rain, and sun.

OUTWITTING
THE GARDENER

Everywhere the best ornamental
grounds that we see are those
in which vines and creepers are
outwitting the gardener.
We can't have enough little vines
and weeds.

—*Frederick Law Olmsted*

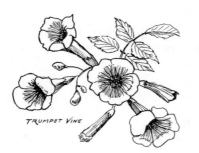

TRUMPET VINE

ANY GARDEN IS SUBJECT TO INVASION. AND THE gardener can wage all-out solarization, fight an occasional battle, or yield—with grace or kicking and cursing, as the case may be—to any number of stealthy incursions. Earth that was filled with floral bloom and plumping vegetables in spring may be choked with weeds come early October, when it's time to remove the tomato vines and their cages. Tall weeds hide the currant bushes. More modest weeds carpet the squash patch and clog the area devoted to irises and columbines. If rain has been plentiful, it's easy to uproot them and place them, along with the tough tomato vines in the wheeled trash can. If dry weather has prevailed, then the best recourse is to clean them out with the mini-tiller. The newly denuded area may then be covered with broken-down cardboard boxes or planted with annual rye grass.

I find, however, that I want to understand my foes. Whence do they come? What are their tribal habits? Are they good for anything at all? I can certainly do without most of them but in several cases, the answer to the last question is Yes—at least in my perceptions. And there's a precept here:

> *Know thine enemy. Become acquainted with the plants that you don't like—dandelions, thistles, plantains, pokeweed, and all the rest that invade your garden like a Mongol horde. All have histories, and many have served human uses. Then, if you still don't like them, root them out.*

Like almost everyone, including the keepers of nearly perfect Lawns, I have been taken hostage by dandelions—and hostage in more ways than one. Common as all get out and well nigh ineradicable, the plant is formally known as *Taraxacum officianale*. It's a Eurasian perennial of the Aster family, with milky juice and a deep, tapering taproot. Because of that hearty root, the Chinese call it "earth nail" and have anciently used it as food and medicine. In Japan, it has figured as an ornamental plant with more than 200 varieties, some of them orange, black, and white in addition to yellow. Until the twentieth century, that country also boasted a national Dandelion Society. The plant's generic name comes from the Greek and means "remedy for disorder." The species designation, "sold in shops," attests to its medicinal usefulness and edibility. Citing not only its common name but also its Latin name, *Dens leonis*—"Tooth of the lion," John Gerard speaks of both properties in his *Herball*:

> Boiled, it strengthens the weake stomacke, and eaten raw it stops the bellie, and helps the Dysentery; especially being boyled with Lentiles; boyled in vinegar, it is good against the paine that troubles some in making of water; A decoction made of the whole plant helpes the yellow jaundice.

The French also called it *dent de lion*, "tooth of the lion," an easily anglicized phrase that refers to its sharply incised leaves.

When and why did it come to the New World? It's not mentioned in early lists of seeds ordered from the Old World or in seventeenth-century descriptions of New England. A writer who has surveyed exotic plants that have made themselves thoroughly at home in North America says, "There was a reason for this. The dandelion was not an economic plant but a common green for the stewpot, a 'dosing herb,' and so its seeds were among those that each woman was expected to take with her for the family garden plot." So dandelion seeds were sown along with those of other simples, like marigolds and scurvy grass (*Cochlearia officinalis*), in gardens protected from rabbits and other raiders by woven fences packed with mud.

Many people think that the dandelion is the vegetable equivalent of the European starling, another introduced species generally loathed in North America. But I like dandelions. The color of the flower takes me hostage, for it cheers me (though if it's springing from a leafy rosette in the vegetable garden, rather than the grassy paths, I grab the dandelion digger). The plant also holds me hostage to memories—waving the bright flower just under someone's chin to get the golden reflection that denotes a fondness for butter; huffing and puffing on the seedhead to send as many little plumed parachutes as possible spinning in the air. The gardener-poet Jeffery Beam has written this of dandelions:

What Man named
the lion's tooth &
Time named Dandy
now Man holds in
low regard.

Bittersweet greens for eating.
Bee's temple of the sun.
Rabbit's common heaven.

Children know your
yellow flowers &
white ghosts.

Though many people continue not only to complain but also to con-
duct outright chemical warfare against dandelions, its greens still
deck dinner tables; bees do sip the abundant nectar; rabbits thrive
on the leaves; and children forever hold dandelions under chins and
puff at the blowballs. The only blessing that the poet fails to mention
is dandelion wine, which is made by fermenting the yellow flowers.
Long live dandelion gold!

The other not-so-weedy weed that brings me great delight is
ground ivy (*Glechoma hederacea*). The binomial means "ivy-like
mint," which refers to the shape of its leaves and to the volatile oil in
glands on the leaves' undersides. And it is indeed a member of the
Lamiaceae, the Mint family (which used to be called the Labiatae, the
Lip family, because its flowers have an upper lip that folds over a
lower lip). Introduced from Eurasia long ago, it's a modestly attractive, ground-hugging, creeping perennial with a square stem and little, round bright-green leaves that have scalloped edges. Its roots are
shallow and may be pulled up easily, but I remove it only when it covers a spot in which I need to dig holes for daffodils and other bulbs.
It has a merry assortment of common names. In addition to ground
ivy, John Gerard mentions Ale-hoofe, Gill go by ground, Tune-hoofe,
and Cats-foot. And, truly, the leaves *are* the size of a small cat's foot.
Mrs. Grieve, author of *A Modern Herbal*, adds Haymaids, Hedgemaids, and Lizzy-run-up-the-hedge to ground ivy's monikers. The
Oxford English dictionary offers Hayhove. Many of these names say
something about the plant's habits or uses. It can cover fields and
climb hedges. Gerard says that, for a reason unknown to him, it was
"tunned up in ale"—that is, put into a large cask of ale. It supposedly
helped to clarify and preserve beer and improve its flavor. These days
it's not an item used in traditional medicine, but once upon a time,
according to Gerard, it was "commended against the humming noyse

and ringing sound of the ears, being put into them, and for them that are hard of hearing."

Being neither an ale-drinker nor a victim of ringing in my ears, I cherish ground ivy for other virtues. For one, its unobtrusive greenness does not fade even in winter. Then, it sends its long, delicate vines tumbling quietly from the terrace down the gray limestone wall to the earth of the lower backyard. I had thought of taking cuttings from the English ivy (*Hedera helix*) that rambunctiously climbs my rose-of-Sharon bushes and covers portions of the chain-link fence, but it's an uppity vine that would eventually hide the wall (though perhaps not in my lifetime). Ground ivy, though modest, is marvelously ornamental.

As for the vines lauded by Frederick Law Olmsted, several inhabit my backyard. My favorite—for the vibrant red-orange color of its blossoms—is trumpet vine, also known as trumpet-creeper (*Campsis radicans*), a plant native to North America. It's one of the Bignoniaceae, the Trumpet-Creeper family, which it shares with the catalpas (*Catalpa bignoniodes* and *C. speciosa*). The family was named in honor of the Abbé Jean Paul Bignon (1662–1723), who was librarian to Louis XIV. Despite its wont, like most vines, to wrap everything else in its lusty embrace, trumpet vine is immensely ornamental. *Campsis radicans*—the genus-name comes from the Greek word for "bent" and refers to the crooked stamens of the flowers, while the species-name indicates that the plant's woody stems are capable of taking root. I contemplate my trumpet vines and shake my head, remembering the Carolinas, where the plant is well and truly a weed, entwining itself through and over fences, climbing rampant up trees and telephone poles. Here, farther north, they have better manners, not intruding where they are not welcome, and should they become a little obstreperous, the pruning shears can put them right smartly in their place. I call them "my" trumpet vines, but they aren't really mine, for but arise in the Luddites' backyard in the foot or so between their shed and the concrete retaining wall that supports my terrace on its north side. I very much doubt that the

Luddites know that they have provided me with treasure—a dense cascade of shiny dark-green leaves concealing vines that are old and large enough to have scaly bark and grand clusters of three-inch-long, tubular flowers that present profuse and gladsome bloom by midsummer. The flowers, flared at the end, look as if they might, at any minute, emit stirring music—"The Saints Come Marching In," "El Mariachi," or a march by John Philip Sousa. In autumn, seed-pods, five inches long and an inch wide, form and turn light brown as they dry; each pod contains a host of winged seeds. The pods can be cut and brought inside to put in a vase, along with cattails, teasel, and dried grasses to make fall decorations.

Two other vines indigenous to the New World have made them-selves at home in my yard, one of them with grace, the other ruth-lessly—Virginia creeper (*Parthenocissus quinquefolia*) and wild clematis or virgin's bower (*Clematis virginiana*). The scientific name of Virginia creeper means "five-leaved virgin's ivy," and it's a mem-ber of the Vitaceae, the Vine family, which includes grapes. Those dark-green leaves, arranged in the shape of a five-pointed star, pos-sess true elegance from the moment that they emerge in spring. In early fall, well before the leaves of most other deciduous vegetation, except for dogwood and black gum, they turn deep red. The event, known as fall foliar flagging, signals birds that fruit is ready. And the feathered tribes alight to feast on drupes and berries. The relation-ship is known as mutualism, a win-win form of symbiosis, in which birds find fuel for their migratory journeys and plants find transport for their seeds. Virginia creeper offers much to admire, and it's easy to keep within bounds.

But virgin's bower, for all that its name bespeaks innocence, is totally immodest, totally grabby. My mother let it climb the iron fence that separated lawn from sidewalk at her house, and it had the delicate appearance of a lacy white bridal veil. There a lawn mower kept it within bounds. But here, if it could, it would leap from its point of origin in the Luddites' unkempt lot and smother the nine-foot-tall rose-of-Sharon bushes that grow on the north side of my backyard, just as it has smothered a small rhododendron at the

Luddites'; it would also clamber over the wall in front and shroud my herbs and the little Japanese maple tree with its labyrinthine tangle of slender vines and snow-white flowers. But it can't smother or shroud, for I trim it back or yank it up with the same ruthlessness that characterizes its mode of growth.

Yet, like all green growing things, it's an interesting plant, which belongs to the Ranunculaceae, the Buttercup family. Translated literally, Ranunculaceae would mean "Family of the Little Frog," *ranunculus* being Latin for "little frog," a creature that likes the damp places also favored by buttercups and their kin. Virgin's bower is considered a wetlands indicator plant, but I haven't noticed that the vine is fond of puddles or wet weather, for in my neighborhood and surely elsewhere, it flourishes right smartly in times of drought. The binomial, *Clematis virginiana*, means "vine from Virginia," with *clematis* being a generic Greek word for "vine." It was introduced to the British Isles sometime in early colonial days, for John Gerard notes it in a chapter called "Of purging Peruinckle." Giving its common name as Virgins Bower, he assigns to it the Latin name *Clematis urens*, "stinging" or "burning" clematis "by reason of his fierie and burning heate, because that being laid upon the skin, it burneth the place, and maketh a schar [scar], even as our common caustick and corrasive medicines do." It is the leaf that supposedly creates the burning sensation and real blistering. Having touched leaves, stems, flowers, and seedpods all too frequently in my campaign against the vine, I have experienced no pain—except the psychic pain of wishing that I didn't have to deal with this pretty but obstreperous and clingy vegetation. Gerard notes that the plant is not found in the wild in England but that he grows it in his garden, where it flourishes. He also provides a long list of common names aside from Virgins Bower and purging Peruinckle: "Biting Clematis, white Clematis, Biting Peruinckle, and Ladys Bower." Nor are these the only common names for the plant. A British book on flower fairies offers Traveller's Joy (using English orthographics) for the vine in bloom, for then it builds "a shady bower to shelter you from the sun or shower," but in fall it's called

Old Man's Beard for the fine white fluff of the flowers going to seed. The profile of *C. virginiana* in the U.S. Department of Agriculture's plants database recognizes the scientific name but not virgin's bower, which is accepted by botanists from John Gerard to the authors of *A Field Guide to Wildflowers* in the field guide series edited by Roger Tory Peterson. The USDA prefers devil's darning needles, a moniker that refers to the dainty yet stiff and needlelike seedpods. The plant, native to or naturalized in all but eleven western states, Alaska, and Hawaii, is well-nigh unstoppable. Even so, I can appreciate its history if not its habits.

An introduced vine also grows willy-nilly in my yard: honeysuckle (*Lonicera japonica*), which originated in east Asia. A member of the Caprifoliaceae, the Honeysuckle family, it was brought to the United States in 1806 as a plant for landscaping. *Lonicera* honors the sixteenth-century German naturalist Adam Lonitzer; *japonica* means "of Japan," where the specimen plant was first collected and named. Since its arrival in North America, it has found suitable habitats in thirty-nine of the fifty states; the only areas into which it hasn't ensconced itself are the upper Midwest and the far West, where frigid winters have kept it from taking hold. In more places than not, it's now deemed a completely undesirable alien. Illinois, for one, forbids the sale and distribution of honeysuckle, Vermont has designated it a noxious weed, and in New Hampshire, it's a prohibited invasive species. By just what means it can be prohibited is unknown to me, for the plant distributes itself without taking the least note of human sanctions. And it uses a fail-safe array of methods to propagate itself: aboveground runners, underground rhizomes, and seeds. Birds, excreting the seeds, are the primary force behind the plant's spread. The problem is that honeysuckle outcompetes native vegetation, discouraging, then obliterating tender annuals and tree seedlings. The only way to get rid of the stuff is killing it along with every other bit of greenery in the area. So, given the impossibility of eradicating *L. japonica* in my yard, for that would eradicate everything else, I've learned to live with it. Goodness knows, it's here to stay, scrambling up from the Luddites' yard, spilling down the limestone drywall and the concrete foundation of the long-gone carriage house, and twining through the chain-link fence. As with the trumpet vines, my only defense is the pruning shears. But it redeems itself with an ineffably sweet fragrance. Honeysuckle's perfume scents the days and nights of early summer. Hummingbirds hover over it and sip; so do the little butterflies known as skippers. And I learn that, like lantana, it communicates with insects. The delicate spurs and fluted corollas of new flowers are decked out bridal white, but a day later, they are as yellowed as old newsprint. The change in color makes for a natural economy of effort, signaling that there's no need for an insect to visit because a blossom that's no longer white has already been pollinated.

Nor are honeysuckle, trumpet vines, Virginia creeper, and virgin's bower the only reaching, stretching, commandeering plants that have made themselves at home in my garden without invitation. Among the sorners—those plants that, like the man who came for dinner, take advantage of the host's hospitality and linger there a decade later—is a member of the Rosaceae, the Rose Family: *Rubus idaeus*, the "bramble from Mount Ida." And a bramble it is, not just because the canes bristle with thorns but also because birds or squirrels have always gotten there first, and I've never managed to harvest the fruit. The canes spill with wild abundance down the neighborhood's hilly backyards. Mrs. Luddite surprised me last year by bringing me a full cup of fruit that she'd picked on her steep back bank—red raspberries, sweet as nectar. It's puzzling that this plant with a shrublike growth should be designated as "from Mount Ida" (though it's certainly at home on Staunton's steep hills). That name is shared by a mountain located on Crete, and a mountain southeast of the ancient city of Troy and renowned as the site at which Paris awarded the golden apple to Venus in a tightly fought beauty contest. But the red raspberry is as American as squash and green beans, which are all delicious gifts from the New World.

I am a maniacal list-maker—shopping lists, book lists, Christmas lists, inventories of the freezer's contents and the furnishings of Tomato Haven. And I keep a garden book, an act that leads to a precept:

A garden book is easy to keep. Fancy, month-by-month versions, with illustrations, are available in stores, but it's not necessary to spend a large amount of money. A spiral-bound notebook will do for a daily record. These are items to list: where and when you buy plants or seeds, what you plant or sow in starter pots, the dates of planting, and, with vegetables, when and how much you harvest. Keeping such a book obviates the tedium of trying to remember when to set in daffodil bulbs or sow cole crops for a fall harvest.

And if I list all these items, why not list the weeds? As with dandelions and daylilies, they have stories.

Like the dandelions, honeysuckle, and ground ivy, most of the weeds in my yard are exotic. They traveled here in all innocence from every part of the world but the polar regions. They came in luggage, on boot soles and animal hooves, by wind, water, and bird. Some, like the dandelion and the common mallow, were collected and brought here intentionally. And here's the roster of immigrants not already mentioned. They were dispersed from whatever Ellis Island served as their port of entry:

- amaranth, also called redroot pigweed, *Amaranthus reflexus*, annual, native to tropical America
- bindweed, field, *Convolvulus arvensis*, perennial, native to Europe
- bristlegrass, green, also called green foxtail, annual, native to warm temperate Asia, North Africa, the Indian subcontinent, and temperate Europe
- burdock, common, *Arctium minus*, biennial, native to Europe

- clover, red, *Trifolium pratense*, biennial or tender perennial, native to North Africa, warm temperate Asia, the Indian sub-continent, and temperate Europe
- henbit, also called henbit dead-nettle, *Lamium amplexicaule*, biennial, native to Europe and Africa
- Indian strawberry, *Duchesnea indica*, perennial, native to Asia
- lady's thumb, *Polygonum persicaria*, annual, native to Europe
- lamb's-quarters, also called pigweed or goosefoot, *Chenopodium album*, annual, native to Eurasia
- mallow, common, *Malva neglecta*, annual or biennial, native to Europe
- morning glory, blue, also called tall morning glory, *Ipomoea purpurea*, annual, native to tropical America
- onion, wild, also called wild garlic, crow garlic, or field garlic, *Allium vineale*, perennial, native to Europe
- sida, prickly, *Sida spinosa*, annual, native to tropical America
- winter cress, also known as yellow rocket, *Barbarea vulgaris*, biennial, native to Europe

Many of these are good for nothing except crashing into gardens like relentless green juggernauts. But even these pushy plants have histories worth relating (though they have inspired poetry only in a generic sense—the lap full of seed, for example, that William Blake cannot sow "without tearing up some stinking weed"). The common mallow, for one, was introduced as an ornamental plant. It is indeed one of the Malvaceae, or Mallow family, that proudly counts flowers and edibles from hollyhock (*Althaea rosea*) and rose of Sharon to okra (*Hibiscus abelmoscha*) among its members. The most economically important member of the family is cotton (*Gossypium* species). The family has its black sheep, too, and the one known formally as *M. neglecta* is the one that infests my garden. It's not hard to see the reason that it was once considered ornamental: the leaves, like those of ground ivy but twice as large, are scalloped rounds, and the tiny flowers bloom white. Its flaw, at least in my opinion, is that it develops a long, skinny, exceedingly tough taproot that's impossible to pull up unless there's been a sozzling, soil-loosening rain. Nor can I extract the common mallow with a dandelion digger, for the severed root reaches so far down in the earth that, with only a little remaining, the plant takes on new life and, like a worm that's been cut in half, regenerates itself, sprouting a whole mess of fresh greenery. It's everywhere an upstart, snuggling under the pepper plants and the horseradish, flourishing beside the lettuce, cozying around the front yard's iris and sage. But John Gerard assigns a host of virtues to the common mallow and its close kin:

> A.   The leaves of Mallowes are good against the stinging of Scorpions, Bees, Wasps, and such like; and if a man be first anointed with the leaves stamped with a little oyle, he shall not be stung at all.
> B.   The decoction of Mallowes with their roots drunken are good against all venome and poyson, if it be incontinently taken after the poyson, so that it be vomited up again.
> C.   The leaves of Mallowes boyled till they be soft and applied, do mollifie tumors and hard swellings.

He also declares that the decoction is good against the "fretting of the guts, bladder and fundament." His list does nothing, however, to change my mind about the common mallow's unworthiness to inhabit my garden. But it's there in abundance. I don't have to like it, but some tolerance is necessary.

Henbit is far easier to deal with. Like ground ivy, it belongs to the Lamiaceae, the Mint family, nor is it difficult to dislodge, for its roots maintain only a gentle grip on mother earth. But I often leave the plant undisturbed (unless it occupies a spot in which I'd rather see beans), for it possesses a certain prettiness, with frilly, stem-hugging paired leaves from which small flowers peep shyly. Because its leaves resemble those of the nettle but do not sting, it's also known as dead-nettle, a word that simply translates the Greek word, *Lamium*, which designates its genus. *Amplexicaule*, the species-name, means "stem-clasping," an apt description of its leaves. Of course, Gerard has something to say about this plant, the name of which he variously spells "Henbit" and "Henne-bit." He classifies it among the "bastard Chickweeds" but recognizes that its leaves do resemble those of the "dead Nettell" and notes its "slender blew floures tending to purple, in shape like those of the small dead Nettle." (Gerard's orthography is, as usual, not rigorous.) Henbit grew in my esteem when, without seeing the connection at first, I purchased several plants that share its genus for setting amid the three dwarf gray-green juniper bushes (*Juniperus*) that occupy a portion of a small bed, fifteen feet long and a yard wide, on the south side of the house. All that I knew when I selected them was that I wanted prostrate perennials to cover the spaces between the little junipers. Behold, they turned out to be *Lamium maculatum*, spotted deadnettle, a ground-hugging plant with variegated leaves of pale green edged with white. Of the five plants put in, four have small white flowers, while the flowers of the fifth are fire-engine red. Common mallow, no. Henbit, yes!

Lamb's-quarters—*Chenopodium album*, "white goosefoot"—a member of the Chenopodiaceae or Goosefoot family, also receives a nod of assent. The family is a large one that includes spinach, beets, carnations, and a host of others. The reason giving the nod to lamb's-quarters? It's edible. As one garden writer puts it, "If you happen to have Lambs-quarters where you don't want it, pull it up or hoe it down before it goes to seed. Better yet, use it for dinner." Truly, it's more than edible—it's delicious! One of its common names is wild spinach, and the only price is fifteen minutes of easy labor. The plant will provide a mess of greens from spring till frost. Gather the leaves that are not tough, boil them briefly, drain, and cover them liberally with pats of butter, which will soon melt. Serve their butter-drenched succulence with a hard-cooked egg and a tad of vinegar. Not only do they taste good, but they're good for you because they are high in vitamins A and C, calcium, potassium, and phosphorus. Nor are we the only creatures that consume lamb's-quarters. Birds, squirrels, and chipmunks eat the seeds, and so do people. Archaeologists have discovered that the plant was cultivated at Iron Age settlements in Denmark, most likely for the tiny but copious seeds, which can be ground into flour and mixed with wheat flour or used whole like poppy seeds.

Winter cress is another edible wild green. Its binomial, *Barbarea vulgaris*, refers to the fact that the plant was once known as the herb of St. Barbara, patron of miners and protector of people caught in thunderstorms. The species-name, "common," testifies to the plant's ubiquity in its European homeland (it is equally at home here in its adopted country). It belongs to the Brassicaceae, the Mustard family, as do broccoli, cauliflower, and the other cole crops. Gather it before winter is out, when it's still young, and add it to a salad for a mildly peppery taste. Or shred the leaves and mix them with onions, vinegar, salt, crisp bacon, and bacon grease. In spring, the leaves become bitter, though that unpleasantness may be removed by boiling the greens twice. But when the plants flower, the leaves become unpalatable. As I write, it's January, and I noticed only yesterday that enough winter cress for a salad has sprung up in the front-yard vegetable patch.

Along with these foreigners, we have the natives, the green intruders that have always been here. In addition to brambles, Virginia creeper, trumpet vine, and the obnoxious virgin's bower, the list includes these:

- bur cucumber, *Sicyos angulatus*, annual
- cinquefoil, common, *Potentilla canadensis*, perennial
- fleabane, eastern daisy, also known as common fleabane, *Erigeron annuus*, perennial
- goldenrod, *Solidago* species, perennial
- nightshade, also called horse nettle, *Solanum carolinense*, annual
- nutgrass, also called chufa flatsedge, *Cyperus esculentus*, perennial, native also to Europe
- plantain, common, also called broadleaf plantain, *Plantago major*, perennial, sometimes annual, native also to Eurasia
- pokeweed, *Phytolacca americana*, perennial
- sicklepod, *Cassia obtusifolia*, annual

- Spanish needles, also called pitchfork, *Bidens bipinnata*, annual
- spurge, spotted, also called small spotted sandmat, *Chamaesyce maculata*, annual
- violet, blue (*Viola* species), perennial
- violet, confederate, also called woolly blue violet, *Viola sororia priceana*, perennial
- wood sorrel, common yellow, *Oxalis stricta*, perennial

Eastern daisy fleabane's scientific binomial enchants me. The genus-name comes from two Greek words—*eri*, which means "early," and *geron*, "old man." "Early old man" sounds unlikely—until you see the new springtime leaves of some species covered with a frost of fine down. All fleabanes are members of the Aster family, and most are perennials, but daisy fleabane's species-name tells that it's annual or biennial. I knew its very similar biennial cousin, common fleabane, sometimes called Philadelphia fleabane, when I lived and gardened in North Carolina. So, when daisy fleabane bloomed in my Virginia yard, I recognized it right away. In maturity, the abundant pale lavender ray-flowers of both species radiate from a golden disk, and the whole is smaller than a dime. But, as it happened, I did not recognize the plant before it became mature. When the squash vines and peppers were at last pulled up, and the last of the sunflowers had dropped its seed-swollen head, I noticed that the vegetable patch was full of earth-hugging dark-green rosettes no bigger than my palm. What could they possibly be? Finding out led to a series of trial-and-error attempts to identify them. In the past, I've not infrequently shipped botanical specimens to extension agents and botanists for identification, but the little rosettes resisted all my efforts to send them safely through the mail. I dug up a batch and sent it off between stiff pieces of cardboard. Word came back: plants so deteriorated that they cannot be identified. I was advised to wrap the roots in damp paper towels and try again. These, too, met with disaster, arriving as mush. A third method was suggested, and it's worth repeating, if ever you have need to mail samples to a botanist:

Carefully dig up the plants including sufficient roots. Gently rinse the dirt from the roots. Lay the plants flat on several layers of newsprint, and cover them with several more layers. Place the works under something heavy—an unabridged dictionary or a pile of pavers. Change the newspapers every day until the specimens are dry. Then, protecting them with cardboard covers, place them in an envelope and mail them.

Off the specimens went. Back came the answer: eastern daisy flea-bane. The problem was telling the difference between the babe and the grown-up. The plant's common name speaks to the now-discredited belief that it repels fleas. Early settlers may well have re-marked on its resemblance to an Old World plant, also known as flea-bane, with a reputation for keeping fleas at a distance. I've also heard it said that the little dark seeds resemble fleas. No matter the reason for the common name, these delicate blooms are so charming that they should be an integral part of any wildflower bouquet in the east-ern half of the United States.

The plant called Spanish needles, yet another member of the Aster family, is another matter altogether. Its immature form is at-tractive, forming a rosette of dark-green leaves variegated with gray-green. But the grown plant is a sneaky opportunist. The tale lies in its name: *Bidens bipinnatus*, "double-toothed bipinnate." In other words, the plant bites. Each of its slender, half-inch-long, one-seeded dark-brown fruits, as close to looking like a needle as makes no never mind, bears barbs or teeth that are used to grab firmly onto anything that brushes past, be it a sock or a shaggy dog. The plant is merely employing a time-tested reproductive strategy, but its relent-lessness has earned it a slew of nicknames, among them beggar's ticks, beggarlice, sticktight, and bur-marigold, the last because its tiny yellow flower does resemble a single marigold. Try combing them out of a dog's fur without stabbing yourself and the dog. Try getting every last one out of your socks. There's a solution, of course, nor does it entail the use of chemicals:

> *Keep noxious weeds cut down to size. Use a weed whacker, a mower, or a scythe. As long as the plant does not bloom and set seed, you're safe.*

So, there's use in Spanish needles, after all: they provide a general precept.

I'm of two minds about the violets, one of which I have not been able to identify precisely—the ordinary-looking violet, with purple-blue flowers. The other, much less in evidence, is the Confederate violet, with charming white flowers streaked with fine purple lines. In spring, both are beautiful. Snuggling around the sedums and at the base of the irises, they bloom extravagantly, wildflowers behaving in a seemingly domestic fashion. But when bloomtime is over, they become gawky, their stems shoot up, and the leaves spread out, obscuring their truly tame neighbors. Without mercy, I chop them back. Then, in fall, they win my affection again, for they put out new flowers.

Love them, love them not, we suffer the weeds. But just as they have their strategies, so do we. And the garden can contain us both.

WOOING THE GREEN MAN,
COURTING DAME KIND

Blessed, the person who knows the
gods of the countryside,
Pan, Silvanus the old man of the
woods, and the sister Nymphs.

—*Virgil*, Georgics, *Book 2, 493–4*

WHAT IS A GARDEN? CAN IT BE DEFINED? ONE notable garden writer asks if a patch of wildflowers in the woods becomes a garden if it's admired or fenced in. She then responds, "The advocate of cultivation would say that unless I *do* something to that bit of land, it remains just nature observed or nature possessed. The intuition here is that a garden must be worked. It needn't be enclosed; it needn't have flowers; it can even look exactly *like* untouched land. But unless someone has shaped and cultivated that land, it isn't a garden." She later lists the six elements essential to garden art: "scale, proportion, unity, balance, rhythm, and focal point." She's right, but I know full well that something is lacking here: an acknowledgment that gardens have minds of their own, that they're inhabited by a nervous green energy, that they are connected not only with poetry but with the divine. And they change willy-nilly, taking the gardener along for the ride.

My friend Donna speaks easily of the energy. "You should see my dog in my garden," she says. "He moves oh so carefully around the plants and bushes." And she imitates the way in which he lifts one paw, then another, with slow precision before moving a mere inch ahead. "He *knows*. He's honoring the Devas. But away from the garden, he's back to his old romping self."

"Devas?" I ask.

"You know—the fairies."

When I was a child, my mother and an aunt read me stories of fairies in gardens, and as an adult I happily own a copy of Cicely Mary Barker's enchantingly illustrated book *The Flower Fairies Changing Seasons*. Pull a tab at the bottom of the page, and the fairy-guarded hazelnut changes its dress from spring catkins to autumn nuts, and the hawthorn, from bouquets of white flowers to clusters of red berries. The fairies change their dresses, too, from April's pastels to fall's deep browns and golds. So, I've known all my life about the association of fairies with gardens. But *Devas*? The word is entirely new to me. I look it up, of course. *Webster's Third* defines a deva as "a divine being or god in Hinduism and Buddhism," notes its etymological connection to "deity," and sends me on to see also *daeva*. That's a Persian term, used by Zoroastrians to denote an evil spirit or a maleficent supernatural being. Like deva, it comes from a Sanskrit word meaning *god*. The idea of malevolence—intentional malice!—in a garden makes me shudder, although every gardener must accept the existence of happenstance and misfortune. I find a better definition in the World Wide Web's *Fairy Encyclopedia*:

> Deva is a word that comes from the Persian and means "shining one." It may once have been a generic term for all faery life, but as the world went west, first to Greece and then to Britain, it became associated with deeply elemental nature spirits. Devas are small faeries who appear as bright spheres of light. They can lie in lakes, trees, or woods and take on elemental vibrations depending on where they choose to live.

Yes, that kind of sprite is as welcome in a garden as a firefly. But there's much more to the idea of invisible presences amid green-growing things than the *Fairy Encyclopedia* suggests. A grand prehistoric event disposes us to sense the divine in flower beds, vegetable patches, meadows, woods, and even in Lawn.

To garden is to participate in rites that have been going on since humankind committed the real Edenic sin, which had nothing to do with an apple and a snake and everything to do with abandoning our hunting-gathering niche in favor of staying put to raise sheep, goats, and cows and to grow wheat and peas. Our sin consisted of flouting biological destiny. And with our new roles came a host of new concerns, all of which acquired divine as well as practical aspects.

Gardens are places rich in numen. They burst with an exuberant green energy and positively vibrate with the unseen forces of growth and decay. Wherever people have lived and worked the earth, they— we—recognize guardians of the green world: deities, tutelary spirits, the elemental powers of nature. We see not them but what they do. The moon tugs at growing seeds, cozening root vegetables down, down into the earth as it wanes, and, as it waxes, pulling above-ground crops up, up into the light. The sun brings blessing and cursing, warmth for growth and rainless heat that desiccates and kills. Bounty and blight walk hand in hand. We personify these phenomena and give them human form.

Often, I think of them in their Roman incarnations. And despite Virgil's deep doubts that piety and prayer can assure a good crop—he believed that the key to success was hard work, and even that was not always enough to fend off weeds, seed-devouring birds, and drought—he nonetheless invokes the gods and goddesses of the Italian countryside. Two are still well known, even in this age that studies computers rather than mythology. One is Ceres, goddess of grain, who introduced agriculture and so helped to end the golden age, when humankind lived without labor on the animals and plants that the land provided. The other is Bacchus, god of grapes and wine. In the second book of the *Georgics*, which deals with trees and grapevines, Virgil issues an invitation that is at once both playful and reverent:

Father of Wine-Making, come! Everything here overflows
with your gifts. For you, the vines are laden in the vineyard,
and the vintage foams in full-to-brimming vats.
Come, Father of Wine-Making, tug off your boots, come with me
to stomp the grapes and dye your bare legs purple in the raw juice.

The two of them, poet and god pressing the juice from the grapes
with their feet, experience a runner's high; they're drunk as lords on
the pleasure of what they're doing, on the anticipation of the vintage
to come.

The other native Italic deities who are summoned to the poem are
less familiar—Liber, who presided over planting and the setting of
fruit; Pales, who watched over shepherds as shepherds watch their
flocks; the Fauns and Dryads, who dance as they guard the fields and
the folds, and Silvanus, the old man of the woods, whose domain was
forests and uncultivated land. His symbol, held like a scepter, was an
uprooted cypress. One deity whom Virgil does not mention is Robigus,
the god whom people implored to keep their crops from being blasted
by blight and smut and rust and wilt. I think of him whenever I see
tomato plants begin to droop and wither just as they are setting fruit.

Roman farmers also consulted celestial signs. When Arcturus
rises, build up the soil with light furrows so that weeds don't
smother the crop. For a harvest of wheat, wait until the Pleiades set
at dawn before committing the seeds to the earth. When Libra makes
the hours of waking equal to the hours of sleep, sow barley in the
fields. They read the stars just as assiduously as people nowadays
look up astronomical and meteorological data in *The Old Farmer's
Almanac* before they sow and reap. That annual publication surely
comprises a gentle irruption of the Past into the Present. In some
ways we haven't changed much at all.

My garden's tutelary spirit arrived in a box that weighed as much as
two bricks and was gaily wrapped in Christmas paper. When I
opened the package, sent by my sister, behold—a Green Man! He
now observes my Garden and its goings-on, and does so from his

vantage point on the outside wall of the shed. To sow and set in seedlings is to solicit his protection. More than that, to garden is to woo him.

Primordial spirit of natural growth, he's been around since time began. The expression on the high-cheeked face of the Green Man in my yard is one of gentle vigilance, and his head is wreathed with acorns and oak leaves. But he has appeared in a thousand other green guises. Silvanus, ancient Italy's Old Man of the Woods, is only one of them, and like him, many Green Men are depicted carrying a club or an uprooted tree. Greece's lusty and goat-footed Pan is another. The Green Man's images are found in cathedrals and churches from England to France and Germany on to Hungary and Cyprus. He occurs on the capitals of Roman columns. He appears in Egypt as Osiris; he is the Sufi prophet Khidr, whose footsteps are green. Sometimes, his features are plump, sometimes gaunt, sometimes merry, and sometimes stern, but they are always foliate. His head sprouts curling leaves, leaves grow boldly from his chin and cheeks, and sometimes leaves erupt like green fire from his mouth. He also goes by many names other than those that I've already mentioned. He's the Wildman and the Woodwose, Robin Hood, Robin Good-fellow, the Green Knight whom Sir Gawain fought, and Jack-in-the-Green who dresses in leaves and goes in procession with Morris Dancers. He's the King of the May, and the King of the Wood. He appears at Chichén Itzá, a decapitated figure with foliage bursting from his neck. His green is the holy color of Islam, the green of Paradise, and Muslims making the pilgrimage to Mecca wear green. In both Indonesia and Nepal, his foliate face is found. Wherever he is, he gives form to the eternal cycle of death and resurrection in the vegetative world. His eternal resurrection is the reason that a figure coming to us out of prehistory has found a welcome by Christianity.

And where is the female principle amid this rambunctious masculinity? Beneath our feet and radiant above us, descending with precipitation, rising with evaporation; it's all around us soaring, swimming, creeping, burrowing, blossoming, and bearing fruit: Nature—Dame Kind—who is often characterized as a mother. Sometimes, the Green Man is her lover; sometimes, her son. There's no struggle here between male and female, between Gaia and the patriarchal heavens that inseminate her with a rush of rain. Green Man and Nature, both are aspects of the same reality.

In my garden I am the female principle, working under the vital and potent tutelage of seeds, sprouts, flowers, and fruit. The work is actually a collaboration between woman and a bursting green energy. My trees shelter Dryads. As for the Green Man, Silvanus, Bacchus, and Pan—they're not to be found in anybody's Lawn. No indeed, for they're all right here by invitation, and I roll in their arms.

A lot of people in Staunton (though not so many as I'd hope for) dedicate their hours, energies, and passions to wooing the Green Man and honoring Dame Kind. In my travels around town, I can't help noticing the Total Gardens and do my best to make contact with their proprietors. My friend Carroll, who has given me the huge golden *Hemerocallis* and several colors of *Tradescantia virginiana*, less beautifully known as spiderwort, knows some of them. Carroll herself is no slouch at bringing floral color to a yard that must be all of an acre on a curving corner of Rainbow Drive. When she and her husband moved there nineteen years ago, not one person on the street grew flowers in the front yard. Carroll says, "I was made to feel like an eccentric because my garden stopped traffic." The real rainbow of Rainbow Drive is in her garden—flowers and more flowers. The grass that's left consists of wide, curving allées between large beds filled with trees and shrubs as well as blossoms, and she knows every one of her plantings by both scientific and common name.

Before we go on a leisurely late-September tour of the garden, we sit in her living room and talk a bit. She tells of a friend who specialized in digging up daffodil bulbs from the yards of deserted houses, and I mention my adventure with kerria. At that, she rises swiftly and goes to a bookcase. The book fetched is a rebound copy of a book once owned by her grandfather, the second edition of *Henderson's Handbook of Plants and General Horticulture*, published in 1890 by Peter Henderson (1822–1890), a plantsman who had his own seed company. Chockful of drawings, it seems to list every plant then known to humankind. Carroll consults it whenever she hears of a green growing thing with which she has little or no familiarity. A large kitchen drawer filled with current garden company catalogues serves as secondary resource—photographs, descriptions, modern scientific names.

"How did you come to be a gardener?" I ask.

"I've been interested in plants all my life," she says. "When I was two, just learning to speak well, I wanted to know the names of the flowers that were growing wild in a ditch near my home—tiger lilies! And when I was very little, I knew that my name was Carroll Louise. My mother would say to me, 'Care,' then, 'Ol.' And I'd repeat what she said. We did the same thing with Lou-eeze. She'd carefully pronounce my whole name and ask me to say it back to her, which I did—Carroll in the Weeds." She's been amid plants ever since.

As we leave the house to amble around in her large garden, much of which is set on a definite incline, she says, "If your yard is steep like mine and too hard to mow, make it into a garden." I give a vigorous nod of agreement. That's advice too little heeded in this hilly town.

The garden in the front yard is fairly level, however, and is set nearly five feet below the level of Rainbow Road. A redbrick wall acts as a foil for lots of greenery. Carroll specializes in flowering perennials, with iris her chief love despite the fact that it is, she says, "too work-demanding." A host of daylilies (*Hemerocallis* species), African daisies (*Arctotis stoechadafolia*) with silver-green leaves, purple-flowered New England asters (*Aster novae-angliae*), and others too many to count keep the irises company. Carroll points out a large-flowered St. Johnswort (*Hypericum pyramidatum*), yarrow (*Achillea* species), peonies (*Paeonia* cultivars), and white-flowered Boltonia (*Boltonia asteroides*) that, with the New England asters, makes a grand fall bouquet. Markers stand by many of the plants so that they can be easily identified no matter what the season. Carroll offers a bit of hard-won knowledge:

*Use pencil on your plant markers because Magic
Marker ink wears off. Write your data—ID, date
purchased, source, anything else that you want to remember—on the back, too.*

The front yard also features a variety of trees and shrubs. Notable among them is a 'Charles Joli' lilac (*Syringia vulgaris*), which
bears profuse and fragrant mulberry-colored blossoms. The binomial means "common lilac"; the genus-name comes from the Greek
word *syrinx*, "pipe," and was given to lilacs because of their hollow
stems. Evergreen American boxwood (*Buxus sempervirens*) grows
nearby. Small Japanese maples spread their low branches modestly
over a raised bed with brick walls. Bird-planted redbuds and a mimosa (*Mimosa* species), a volunteer salvaged from a ditch, grow in
front as well. The yard's prize tree is set near the walk to the house—
a weeping cherry (*Prunus subhirtella*) that was given in thanks by a
German girl who once stayed with Carroll and her family. Carroll's
son planted it. I try to gauge its size—a good thirty feet tall, with a
crown spread of at least twenty. "When it blooms," Carroll tells me,
"it's covered with a pink froth."

We head around toward the backyard. Halfway there, an enormous perennial begonia (*Begonia grandis*) salutes us with a silent
flourish of its trumpet-shaped pink flowers. A sweet bay magnolia
(*Magnolia virginiana*) lifts its glossy dark-green leaves over our
heads. I ask Carroll if she keeps a garden book. "No, but I probably
ought to," she says. "I do take a lot of photographs."

The back is as filled with wonders as the front, and it has a
woodsy feel because of the many trees and shrubs growing there.
Some are gifts from the birds—several slender sassafras trees (*Sassafras albidum*) with their mitten-like lobed leaves, wild persimmons
(*Diospyros virginiana*), many dogwoods (*Cornus florida*), their leaves

now turning red, an elderberry (*Sambucus canadensis*), and a spice-bush (*Lindera benzoin*) decked with many bunches of bright red berries. When I pluck a leaf and crinkle it, a deliciously spicy per-fume makes me sniff the air with great appreciation. Carroll has seen numerous spicebush swallowtail butterflies hovering over this shrub in the summer; they lay their eggs on its leaves, which serve as food to the new-hatched caterpillars. Other backyard trees and shrubs were planted intentionally, among them a large Southern magnolia (*Magnolia grandiflora*), a pin oak (*Quercus palustris*), and a beauty berry (*Callicarpa americana*) now fully decked out with electric-purple berries, which cardinals and other birds relish. There's also a white pine (*Pinus strobus*). Carroll says that she would never again plant white pine—"It's bad in the garden because branches break off in wind storms. And it's so big that it blocks my view of the Blue Ridge." Two towering Eastern hemlocks (*Tsuga canadensis*) make me think of Longfellow's forest primeval where "murmuring pines and the hemlocks stand like Druids of eld" and wonder if hemlocks still flourish in those ancient woods. The hemlocks that grace Carroll's yard must be sprayed twice a year to prevent infestation by the wooly adelgid (*Adelges tsugae*). Since it reached this country in 1924, prob-ably from Asia, this sap-sucking insect has killed thousands on thou-sands of trees. I've seen an infestation. White cocoons too many to count lie at the bases of the needles and make the tree look as if it's covered with tufts of wool.

The wooded area shades one of Carroll's two compost heaps; the other, the one that she stirs with a spading fork, lies near a corner of the house. Neither is confined to a bin, each consists simply of mounded plant matter. Both illustrate entropy: no matter how many clippings, weeds, and spent perennials are added to a heap, it re-mains knee-high. How swiftly vegetation decays! And both heaps are characterized by the rich dark-brown color of humus.

A little farther around the bend is a corner, which gives a home to a grand array of orange flowers, such as orange marigolds (*Taygetes patula*), orange snapdragons (*Antirrhinum majus*), or-ange crocosmia (*Crocosmia aurea*), and orange lion's ear (*Leonotis leonurus*). That last binomial means "lion-colored lion's ear." The orange corner also contains inorganic but necessary items—a birdbath, a rain gauge that's checked once a month, and a blue gazing globe. Another gazing globe, this one golden, rests at the edge of the woods. Nearby, moonflowers (*Ipomoea alba*) cover an arched trellis with their big white blossoms and heart-shaped dark green leaves. They're a contrary sort of morning glory that chooses to bloom not in the day's early hours but rather in the late afternoon, and the blossoms stay open all night.

We walk on. *Plip plip!* Very small frogs leap from the surrounding stones into a very small pool. The pool was built years ago by Carroll's husband, a retired professor of Classics now basking on the house's back deck. A mystery tree shades the pool. Though she has scoured the available books on trees, Carroll has not been able to identify it. The bark on the trunk is gray and fissured vertically, while the newer wood is a reddish brown embellished with small tan bumps. We cut a branch, which I'll send off to my friend the botanical librarian. He, too, is puzzled—the specimen is inadequate—but says that it's probably one of the locusts (*Robinia* species).

The tour ends in the area that Carroll calls "the back forty." Here are the end-of-season remains of a small vegetable patch, which produced cucumbers, tomatoes, and beets in the summer. One yellow cucumber and a lone beet still lie on the ground. "I know what I was going to do here," Carroll says, "but I haven't done it yet—make an Italian-style garden with a large circle in the middle and walks leading to each of four points." Each quadrant will be characterized by its own tutelary tree, all of which are already in place at the farthest possible remove from the circle-to-be. A tulip poplar (*Liriodendron tulipifera*) reigns in one quadrant, while a flowering wild plum with purple leaves (*Prunus subcordata*), a dogwood, and a sarvisstree (*Amelanchier laevis*), which some call service berry, preside respectively over the other three.

Our tour is done. Mopping our foreheads, we head for the house for drinks of cold water. Despite the fact that it's early autumn, the day has been bright and humid. But before I go, we talk briefly about our prime enemies—weeds and bugs. And when it comes to bugs, Carroll offers a truly useful precept:

> *Plant evening primrose* (Oenothra biennis). *Japanese beetles love it. They'll eat it all up and leave everything else alone.*

Trap cropping—aha!

Carroll introduces me to another Total Gardener, Joann, who has rented the first floor of an old house on New Street for the last six years. New Street is filled with Victorian dwellings as closely set together as those in my neighborhood. The one in which Joann lives was built in 1871, when New Street really was new. It abuts the sidewalk on two sides. Garden, and nothing but garden, extends away from the street on the other two sides of the house. Carroll and I arrive on a relatively cool August afternoon. A comfortably round woman in her late fifties with silver beginning to streak her dark hair around her face, she welcomes us heartily. And off we go, accompanied through the grounds by Pound Dog, a middle-sized beige terrier type, and Miss Starbucks, a very small black cat (no cream at all in her black coffee).

The garden is an amazing agglomeration of the wild and the tame, the intentionally sown and the volunteer. Nasturtiums (*Tropaeolum majus*) in an array of bright colors—red, yellow, white with dark purple spots—grow by the side of the house. Climbing vigorously up a tree behind them and sprawling over them are large-leaved vines with big yellow blossoms, definitely one of the Cucurbitae, the Gourd family, and we discover then and there that the vines do indeed bear gourds, small yellow ones with a crooked neck and a dark-green blossom-end. Joann does not always know what will spring up in the yard, but she offers a precept:

Let things grow and discover what they are.

The garden includes some grass, yes, but it winds in yard-wide paths between the giant beds. I'm told that its sinuous nature has driven the landlord to rage. He complained so loudly and bitterly about the difficulties of mowing around curves and protuberant beds that Joann now takes care of that chore. But she's steadily reducing the areas covered by grass. Ground ivy (*Glechoma hederacea*), my favorite weed, completely covers one section that's bigger than my front yard.

The principle behind Joann's garden is that of keeping it natural. The lilacs and one or two of the trees were purchased, and a few plants, like the gourds, nasturtiums, and zinnias, were intentionally sown. Several others, like a nine-foot goldenrod (*Solidago* species) from Carroll's garden, were gifts. But much of Joann's greenery consists of wild, native volunteers. Pokeweed (*Phytolacca americana*) reaches up beside the house as high as the eaves; its stems are dark pink, and soon its berries, now pale green, will turn purple. Cardinals relish them. And people enjoy the new, tender leaves, boiled or steamed, but beware the roots and mature stalks, for they are poisonous. The biennial mullein (*Verbascum* species) has already spent its yellow blossoms this year; the tall brown stalks rise from furry gray-green leaves. But Joe-Pye weed (*Eupatorium purpureum*), a perennial native to eastern North America, has exploded silently into huge, round clusters of rose-pink blossoms. Joann's specimens are only a modest four feet tall, but the plants can shoot up ten or more feet. It is said that the weed, which does not seem at all weedy, is named for one Joe Pye, a Native American. Folk medicine uses its roots as a diuretic tea. To this day, some Native Americans believe that the plant has aphrodisiac powers. Queen Anne's lace (*Daucus carota*), introduced from Europe and widely naturalized, lifts its delicate white parasols in every bed. It can be cut for beautiful bouquets. So (despite my antipathy for the plant) can the silky seed plumes of wild clematis, which Joann calls autumn clematis because the plumes form in the fall. Its small four-petaled white flowers are blooming now. And it's an ardent climber, covering walls, fences, shrubs, and, in Joann's yard, an arbor vitae.

One Eurasian exotic has a prominent place in Joann's beds: the Canadian thistle (*Cirsium arvense*). Leaves and the erect stems, four feet tall, bristle with spines, but the flowers, shaped like little shaving brushes, blush sweetly pink. "I should pull it out," Joann says, "but the birds love the seeds." In her view, Canadian thistles have a use, after all, but the so-called "thistle seed" that goldfinches and juncos devour comes not from a thistle but from an Ethiopian plant called nyjer. When Joann hears this, she vows to cut it down. Another species not usually found in a Southern garden grows nearby. Shooting at least fifteen feet straight up in the air, a lone box elder (*Acer negundo*) sports pinnate leaves attached not to branches but to its slender trunk, which is only as big around as a fifty-cent piece. Native to the U.S., it's a member of the maple family, and one that's often looked down upon as if it were a stepchild, for it does not grow with grace—just imagine that pole with sparse leaves in Joann's garden—and its wood is of poor quality. Nonetheless, the tree has its virtues. The great American ornithologist Elliot Coues (1842–1899) said this about the tree he called *Negundo aceroides*, the "maple-like chaste tree," "The sap yields a fine white sugar, but it is not so sweet as that of the real maple, and more is required to make the same quantity of sugar."

Other trees and shrubs rise amid the flowers. When I make my first visit in August, several redbuds are heavily decked with four-inch-long pods plump with seeds and attached directly to the trees' trunks and branches—no stems, they just sprout straight out of the wood. Butterfly bushes (*Buddleia* variety) wave their erect clusters of pink flowers, and the dogwoods wear green berries, soon to turn red. They are joined by a flowering crab with purple leaves (*Malus* species) and two evergreens, one of them arbor vitae (*Thuja occidentalis*) and the other, a pine species for which Joann doesn't know the common name. No matter, it's a light bright-green with very bushy needles, and we can almost see it growing—four years ago it was a pint-sized pine, but today it's taller than a basketball star, though far more pudgy. The lilacs grow in the garden's lower portion. The leaves are covered with powdery mildew, and Joann confesses that she neglected to spray them this year. She gives her recipe for repelling mildew and bugs:

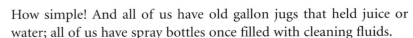

Add two tablespoons of liquid dish detergent to a gallon of water. When the ingredients have been mixed, put them in a plastic spray bottle and apply the mixture lightly to both the tops and bottoms of the leaves. Apply it to vegetables, as well, to discourage insect pests like cabbage butterflies that like to lay their eggs on the undersides of leaves.

How simple! And all of us have old gallon jugs that held juice or water; all of us have spray bottles once filled with cleaning fluids.

On my second visit only two days later, my eye is drawn to a host of things that I hadn't seen the first time around. Like my garden, Joann's is filled with inorganic treasures. She collects rusty metal—an augur, an old hand-plow, a whatzit with curling iron petals that looks for all the world like a sunflower. A peach-colored ceramic cat with blue tiger stripes sits ready to pounce under a patch of Queen Anne's lace. Of course, there are birdbaths, four of them. And lanterns hang from the lower branches of trees. "They're lovely in fall," Joann says, and I vow to come to see them then. Nor are the creature comforts of people neglected. Two old metal chairs, the kind you can bounce in gently (none of this come-lately, immobile plastic stuff) sit by a large, round iron table set close to the ground in a secluded bend.

The most attractive element of the whole garden is one that I hadn't noticed on my first visit. Joann had to point it out. Her garden is entered by a path from the ordinary city sidewalk, and when one steps upon the path, one also passes underneath an extraordinary arch. It looks at first as if it's a wooden affair that supports a very leafy vine. But no, wood and leaves, it consists of one living red maple tree (*Acer rubrum*). A few years ago, Joann spotted a volunteer and, in accord with her wont to let things grow and then discover what they are, left it alone. Staying slender, it stretched upward seeking the sun. And Joann experienced a Eureka moment: the tree could be bent over and fastened to the ground on the other side of the path. A six-foot man might have to duck, but she and I don't.

Joann is definitely, unashamedly wooing the Green Man.

So is Juliette (though she has a perfectly good husband). But his job is to mow what little grass is left in the capacious, down-sloping yard on East Beverley Street—a patch on either side of the front walk and a small, almost circular green in back that consists mainly of ground ivy. The rest is shrubs, trees, ground covers, and flowers, flowers, flowers in curving beds. And it's all hers to tend.

She and her husband have made the house in which they live into an elegant bed-and-breakfast that has been operating since 2000, the year that they moved in. The brick house, designed by a noted local architect and built in 1904, exemplifies a modified prairie style with wide porches. Juliette was destined for running a bed-and-breakfast, for she grew up in a hotel in England, and a delight in gracious hospitality has been with her for all of her days. I'm aware of her welcoming personality as she greets me with a firm handshake and a smile. And off we go on a garden tour. Two kittens, one a blue tabby, the other a silver tabby, both with white, leap, bound, and pounce through the gardens with us. Ten months old, they are sister and brother; she is Portia, and he, Lear, which Juliette's English-bred voice pronounces as "Leah."

Juliette herself has planted some of the trees and shrubs, and some are legacies put in by the people from whom Juliette and her husband purchased the house. The front yard boasts four handsome legacies in the form of yellowwood trees (*Cladastris lutea*), which are native to the South. Slow-growing ornamental shade trees, they bear large white flowers in the spring. The former owners also planted three varieties of boxwood (*Buxus* species): American, English, and Korean. The last displays the dark green leaves of English box but has a more compact form of growth. Then there's the Southern magnolia, once a tree but now a bush. In despair about the tree's unceasing avalanche of leaf-litter, Juliette cut it back severely. Now, only six feet tall, the bush is covered densely with huge, shiny dark green leaves all the way from the ground to its top. Volunteer redbuds and black locust trees (*Robinia pseudoacacia*) lend their cool green shade to the lower yard. A bald cypress (*Taxodium distichus*) grows there, too; it's an evergreen that's not evergreen, for it sheds its needles every fall and puts them out anew, come spring. A fig (*Ficus carica*) lifts its three-lobed, glossy leaves near a Japanese cutleaf maple; the fig was a gift from a friend, a ficophobe, who bought a house with the tree already installed in the yard but, heaven forfend, didn't want to put up with an annual mess of spoiling fruit. And Juliette's trees include a twisting whirl of Harry Lauder's walking sticks (*Corylus avellana* 'Contorta') halfway down the back slope, but they are, alas, as leafless as they'd be in winter—victims of anthracnose, a fungal disease. It may be, however, that they'll recover, as many stricken trees do without human or chemical help.

Juliette has built steps and paths to make the climb up and down the steep backyard easy for guests (and people, like me, with creaky knees)—wide paths with railings, narrow paths with slate steps, and one path that looks like a dry riverbed, with white gravel overlaid with real, water-rounded rocks. The paths are lined with beds in which intentionally set-in plants like *Liriope muscari* share space with volunteers like poke and Joe-Pye weed. Eyecatchers abound: electric and solar lanterns, a blue reflective globe midway down the hill, and a three-level pool with a waterfall. The three basins are host to waterlilies (*Nymphaea* species), yellow iris (*Iris pseudocoras*), and arrowhead (*Sagitarria* species). Koi, one a deep red, swirl through the water, which tumbles from one basin to the next with a quiet, soothing rush. Near the uppermost basin, a flat piece of ground has been paved with flagstones—a perfect corner for a double swing with a canopy. Juliette points out the hyacinth vine (*Dolichos lablab*) winding up one of the swing's supports. It's bearing small, fragrant blossoms of pink, lavender, and white. Sometimes it's called hyacinth bean or Indian bean, and it is indeed a climbing bean that produces edible seeds and pods—purple but edible all the same. I find myself filled with desire for *D. lablab* and a trellis on which it may grow.

Then, on the lowest portion of the yard, avatars of the Green Man appear—two guardian angels, wings unfurled above their heads. Gazing over the lowest portion of the yard, their visages are mounted, one on each side, of a great stone archway that leads into the cool green shadow of a wooded area. I acknowledge them with a nod of my head.

On the way back up, Juliette pulls weeds—grass, ground ivy—as we go, and stuffs them into a covered trash bin set for that purpose beside the path halfway up the hill. Lear and Portia gambol upward on the paths and through the plants, a merry twosome. Before I go, Juliette delivers a precept:

If a plant produces something, be happy. Otherwise, leave it alone.

She tells me, too, that working with her garden has led to a landscaping job on the other side of town—a cottage garden in the fashion exemplified by Anne Hathaway's garden in Stratford-upon-Avon.

Later to be the site of a new B-and-B, it now serves as a grand floral gateway to the Newtown Historic District. The Green Man is finding welcome all over town.

It's in Newtown, on one of its streets named for a president, that I find someone with an astonishing resemblance to the Green Man. His name is Steve, and snow-white hair as thick as foliage curls around his face, sprouts lush from his eyebrows, and falls in an unruly beard from his jaws and chin. Near the front door of his 1870's brick house, the image of the Green Man's kissing cousin, Bacchus, is mounted on the wall. Bacchus's visage is solemn, but you know what he's thinking, for grapes wreathe his head. He's a tutelary presence over Steve's house and his truly Total Garden. And it's clear that both he and Steve are in league with Dame Kind.

I've saved visiting Steve's garden until he and I have finished lunch down at the town's old railroad station, now home to restaurants and antique shops. Autumn, Steve's classic brown tortie cat, greets us as we emerge from my car. Her name is appropriate in two ways, for she wears the warm colors of autumnal leaves, and I meet her on a bright blue day in October. The houses in this part of hilly Newtown are set even more closely together than they are in mine, and the yards are far smaller than those on my street. There may be ten feet or fewer between the sizeable two-story houses on the block. Property lines sometimes go right to the walls of next-door houses. Steve's lot ends only six inches from the house just to the north. A limestone retaining wall separates the sidewalk from his front yard, which is close to five feet above street level.

Steve has been gardening all of his life. The son of a Presbyterian minister, he grew up in Iowa and so knows much about growing corn and soybeans. His family also grew vegetables in a rented plot in a community garden. But Steve's love is flowers. There's nary a vegetable to be seen in his yard.

After he moved here, the garden began in the front yard—a rock garden. It's now a colorful mix of perennials like St. Johnswort (*Hypericum* species). "I'm not good at knowing the names of everything, but I know St. Johnswort, and I love its eccentric flowers." Eccentric they are—bright yellow flowers with bushy stamens and little black dots on the petals. White anemones (*Anemone japonica*) are in full autumnal bloom. A small, earth-hugging gray-green stonecrop (*Sedum* species) peeks out from under the leaves of the anemones and St. Johnswort. I have the same plant in my front yard; where it touches ground, it roots and spreads. And irises thrust up their leafy green blades everywhere. They're favorites, and Steve has planted both bearded types and beardless Siberian irises (*Iris siberica*) on all four sides of his house.

A flagstone patio sits in a squared-off angle between front room and kitchen. An old-fashioned iron bench with wooden seat and backrest invites lingering. A narrow rectangular bed between the terrace and the house is luxuriant with ferns. Steve points out a Japanese painted fern (*Athyrium niponicum* 'Pictum') with gray-green leaves and dark red stems. It's beautiful, and he kindles my desire to plant at least one on my shady terrace when he says, "It's extremely hardy. It can take all kinds of cold weather." A trumpet creeper climbs a wooden trellis on the terrace's north side and serves to shield it from the house next door. A gloriously large Korean cherry tree (*Prunus japonica*) shades the bench and flagstones. Steve acquired it by trading with the proprietor of a local landscaping firm. The price: one prize tree for two nativity scenes from his vast collection. This event suggests a precept:

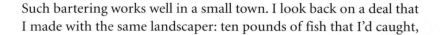

> *If a dealer has a plant that you covet, survey your talents and worldly goods to see what you can offer. No money need change hands.*

Such bartering works well in a small town. I look back on a deal that I made with the same landscaper: ten pounds of fish that I'd caught, cleaned, and frozen for the live Norway spruce now reaching toward heaven in my own backyard.

We go through the house into the backyard. En route he shows me some of his collections—not just nativity scenes but many masks made of clay or wood. The Bacchus on the front porch is just an introduction to the rest. Steve also points out a Hmong story cloth, which tells the tale of a tiger who ate a man and assumed the man's place in life until people got wise to the impersonation and did him in. The faces, garments, and tiger fur are intricately stitched with fine threads, placed so close together that none of the underlying fabric is visible. Autumn the cat lets me stroke her, and she purrs.

Outside again, I see that an earthen path wide enough for two people to walk abreast lies between the house and a three-foot high retaining wall made of railroad ties. "When I came here," Steve says, "the earth lay up against the house several feet deep. You couldn't get out the back door. I had it moved away and built the walls. Found out then that someone must have had a garden here—the soil was good black dirt, not like the stony red clay you find around here." Above the wall, Steve has laid an oval patio of white gravel, upon which he's placed an inviting bench. At patio's front, just above the wall, several impatiens lift their blooms—white and red. Nor are white and red the only colors; this variety may be had in a grand range from white through salmon, orange, and purple to bicolors, and its leaves may come in variegated combinations that include pink and red. I've never before seen such enormous flowers—a good two inches across—on any impatiens. I learn that the variety (*Impatiens x hawkeri*) was discovered in 1970 by plant explorers from Longwood Gardens, founded by Pierre S. du Pont and located in Kennett Square, Pennsylvania. Under the sponsorship of the U.S. Department of Agriculture, the explorers visited New Guinea, where they found it growing in native villages, where it had been cultivated as an ornamental. Plant geneticists at Longwood hybridized the plant and came up with a good number of cultivars, including one named 'Trapeze' that is extraordinarily heat-resistant and drought-tolerant. Cultivation of the New Guinea impatiens was turned over to commercial growers in 1978. The plants may be propagated from seed or cuttings, but only for private use, for the cultivars have been patented. Looking at Steve's array, I find myself trying to envision a spot in my garden for such bold blossoms.

His favorite plants are set along the back property line—three large butterfly bushes (*Buddleia davidii*), each with a different color of blossom—white, lavender, purple. The spelling of the genus name lies under some doubt: Some, including the people who write catalogue blurbs, would have it as it's spelled above, while others would write *Buddleja*. With scientific nomenclature often based on anglicized versions of Latin and Greek, I see no justification for that silent *j*, But the origins of both genus-name and species name are certain. The shrub in one form or another has wide distribution throughout the world; it is native to the Far East, Africa, and South America. When the first specimen was brought to England in 1774, the taxonomists decided to honor the memory of the Reverend Adam Buddle, an amateur who did his botanizing in the 1600s. The species *davidii* came to London's Kew Gardens from China in 1896; that name refers to Père Armand David, a French missionary to China, for whom Père David's deer is also named. "I love those bushes, and not just for the butterflies," Steve says. "When you cut them all the way back, right down to the ground, they grow up again with great vigor." They do need hard pruning each spring. As long as the roots survive, there will be strong new shoots. The butterfly bushes are as enthusiastic as Steve.

Total Garden, yes! As I leave, I realize that if there's one single blade of grass in Steve's yard, I haven't spotted it. Dame Kind is surely pleased.

Each of the gardens that I've visited has its own style. Joann specializes in wildflowers and volunteers, Carroll dotes on floral color, Juliette on plant-shapes and shades of green, and Steve offers small, tranquil, well-shaded spaces limned by trees, shrubs, and flowers. Only Carroll grows vegetables, but she does not focus on them. These people have taken to heart the practice that I've heard called "yardening"—turning a yard completely into a garden. I glance at other Total Gardens as I move about town. One is found in the front yard of a house set well back from the street; most of the yard has been converted into a wide driveway, where often more than one car is parked, but on all sides, shrubs, ornamental grasses, black-eyed Susans, and purple coneflowers bloom. Another Total Garden almost tumbles down a precipitous front yard until it reaches a lime-stone retaining wall that rises five feet above the sidewalk—bamboo, dusty miller, iris, lilies, small evergreens that are decked in lights at Christmastime. It looks as if you'd need scaffolding or a crane to keep from sliding to the sidewalk when setting in plants anywhere on its steep slope. And I can't forget the summertime Total Garden in the tiny front yard of a rental house at the bottom of the hill on which I live: tomatoes, tomatoes, tomatoes. The town's most spectacular Total Garden, located a block west of Joann's, fills the minuscule front yards of a set of seven high-ceilinged, two-story row houses. Giant sunflowers rise almost to the roofs of the columned porches, which feature woodwork sporting scrolled Victorian gingerbread. Hanging baskets filled with red begonias and purple fuchsias compliment the gingerbread. Marigolds glow like little suns at the sunflowers' feet. It is the gardener, a waiter at the best Italian restaurant in town, who updates me on Joann's story. Passing by her house four months after she gave me garden tours, I saw that the garden had disappeared. Nothing at all was left, not a flower stalk, not a lilac bush, not a redbud nor a pine. The red-maple arch at the garden's entrance had been felled. Joann, seeking to escape the town's frigid winters, had found a new home for Miss Starbucks the cat, packed Pound Dog into her van, and taken off for Baja California. At that, her landlord bushhogged the works. "That stupid landlord," says the waiter, "that stupid, stupid man." But he and I both know that Joann will make a Total Garden wherever she may be.

We woo the Green Man's boundless energy, we court Dame Kind, and all in our own ways. They respond, though not invariably as we might hope. The groundhog eats the cucumbers; the squirrels pick and play with baby eggplants; Japanese beetles and earwigs feast on the leaves of the roses. Blights and borers, snails and slugs wreak havoc. Seeds fail to sprout. Yet, good fortune comes along more often than not, and serendipity is ever a part of trying to encourage bloom and fruit. If we are willing to get our hands dirty again and again, we succeed. Wild and elusive as he sometimes seems, the Green Man is not in business to break our hearts. And Dame Kind's genius surrounds us like hard spring rain, like hot summer sun, fall's rustling colors, and the contemplative chills of winter. We come and go. They remain.

GARDEN DREAMING

Gardening is the slowest moving of
the performing arts.

—*Lynden Breed Miller*

N THE COLD MONTHS, GARDENS ARE AS PRESENT AS
they are in other seasons. Fall brings its own imperatives: uproot
tomato vines, fold and store the cages, clip back the bushy
oregano, harvest the last vegetables, till the soil, sow annual rye grass.
These actions are all a part of winding down, of putting the garden
to bed and wishing it sweet dreams before winter covers it with a
quilt of snow. I do these things and look back into a summer now
gone forever. But the looking back holds no sadness, for kitchen
shelves are laden with jars of canned beans and tomatoes, and the
freezer with packages of broccoli, cauliflower, and carrots. I've also
taken many color photographs of the gardens as they change from
spring through fall. Herein lies a precept:

*To accompany your garden journal, take photos fre-
quently and mount them in albums. You'll have a
fine visual record of the garden's year from seedlings
to flowers and fruit.*

I leaf through my albums and trace the garden's progress as it has emerged, bit by bit, from the grass.

I'm looking forward, too. When April with its sweet showers next pierces the drought of March to the root, what shall I see?

✣ DAFFODILS

Last May, seduced by a colorful come-on posted on the Internet, I ordered one hundred daffodil bulbs (*Narcissus* species), a mixed collection appropriate to Zone 6. To think of Wordsworth's "host of golden daffodils" is to think inside a nineteenth-century box. The collection's variety was astounding—white petals around white cups with orange rims, yellow petals around yellow trumpets, white around pink, yellow around orange, large flowers and small. In early September, a patch of earth on the terrace was prepared to receive them. They would find a good home near the 'King Alfred' daffodils descended from those in my husband's father's North Carolina garden. In mid-September, the bulbs arrived in a large cardboard box with holes for ventilation cut into the sides. It must have weighed all of fifteen or sixteen pounds, more than I could easily lug. When I opened the box, I was both pleased and dismayed. First, every bulb was plump, and almost every one had sprouted good-sized daughters. Not just one set of leaves and blossoms but two or three would spring up where each bulb was planted. Second, when the order was placed, I had not the faintest conception of just how many bulbs the number one hundred represented. It looked as if there were at least a thousand. Where to put such unlooked-for abundance? Before I went up to the terrace, bulbs were set around the edges of the front yard's south side and at the base of the limestone wall around the feet of the big metal crane, as well as beside the bin filled with compost and worm castings. Seventy bulbs left to go, and they were still more than I could comfortably carry. Out with a five-gallon bucket, in with fifteen bulbs, and I was set to go. Digging holes six inches deep, placing bulbs therein, and covering them up defines *labor*.

Nonetheless, I persisted, planting all but the last sixteen, which were given away to members of my exercise class.

Daffodils—where do they come from? What is their lore? They're native to northern Europe. John Gerard recognizes and describes twenty-four different kinds of daffodils in his *Herball* and also lists five "bastard daffodils," as well as eight other types, including one that looks like an upside-down hoopskirt surrounded by six tiny petals (modern *N. bulbicodium*). Botanists often used the word *bastard* in Gerard's day; it sometimes meant "inferior," but the *Herball*'s woodcuts show large-trumpeted flowers that we easily recognize as the real thing. Just the same, Gerard dismisses the bastard varieties simply because they are ordinary; he writes of one of them, "The common yellow Daffodill or Daffodowndilly is so well known that it needeth no description." Back then (as well as now) they came in a host of colors—white or yellow petals and cups, purple or saffron coronas.

Gerard does not fail to mention the myth of Narcissus, who was told that he'd live for a very long time if he never looked upon his own face. But he scorned the nymph Echo, whereupon the gods wreaked vengeance, causing Narcissus to gaze at his own image in a pool of water. He fell in love with the unattainable reflection and pined away. When he died, heartbroken, his body turned into the flower that bears his name. The botanist quotes the Roman poet Ovid (43 B.C.–c. A.D. 17), who wrote about this metamorphosis, and gives a late sixteenth-century translation: "But as for body none remain'd; in stead whereof they found / A yellow floure, with milk white leaves ingirting of it round." Gerard also notes the medicinal properties of daffodils. Mixed with honey, the plant can be applied like a plaster to heal a burn and "being stamped with the meale of Darnell and honey, it draweth forth thorns and stubs out of any part of the body." Gerard also warns that eating the roots or drinking a liquid made from them can make you vomit. And that may explain the reason that squirrels find them unpalatable, although those unrepentant rascals may dig them up to knock around as they did my eggplants. But, so far, so good; the bulbs have not been disturbed. And good, sozzling rains have fallen to help their roots take hold.

⋇ WINTER ACONITES

Along with roots, garden dreaming takes hold: What will the yard, especially the terrace, look like come spring? It's not yet Indian summer, we haven't had a black frost, but I envision daffodil colors surging amid the dormant hostas and daylilies and washing up like a pastel tide against the stone walls. A fever seizes me then—plant bulbs and more bulbs. I reread Elizabeth Lawrence's book *The Little Bulbs*. I also go questing in the gardens of memory: behold, small yellow flowers peeping through the February snow! They are winter aconites (*Eranthis hyemalis*—"winter earth-flowers"), a Eurasian plant for which John Gerard specifies the common name of "Winter Wolfes-bane." He writes, "Whole leaves come forth of the ground in the dead time of winter, many times bearing the snow upon the heads of his leaves and floures; yea, the colder the weather is, and the deeper that the snow is, the fairer and larger is the floure."

I check the catalogues and, to my joy, discover that aconites are not expensive. An order for thirty bulbs is placed. When they arrive less than a week later, they surprise me with their tininess—they're no bigger than large peas. Using a dibble, I make holes in the terrace for the length of the limestone wall, drop the small bulbs in, and cover them with peat moss and fallen hackberry leaves.

⋇ SIBERIAN SQUILLS

This is no time to stop! Riding the powerful green wave of garden dreaming, I order twenty-five blue-flowered Siberian squills (*Scilla sibirica*), eight hellebores of mixed colors (*Helleborus orientalis*), and two fritillaries, one yellow (*Fritillaria imperialis lutea maxima*), one red (*F. imperialis rubra maxima*). Siberian squills, which also bear the common name 'Spring Beauty', are members of the Liliaceae, the Lily family, and originated in Eurasia. The name of their genus is a

Roman transliteration of ancient Greek, although in classical times it referred to a shore-loving plant of another genus, now called the sea-onion. It is Elizabeth Lawrence who lures me to the kind that aren't sea-onions. "The delightful thing about squills," she writes, "is that they are so blue, and the most intense blues of all are found in the flowers of *Scilla sibirica* and *S. bifolia*, those two tiny ones that bloom so early in the year and look so brilliant against the rain-darkened earth." And she mentions the "faint underlying tinge of rose on the inside" of the flowers. The Siberian squills, the earliest in the genus to flower, bloom here in February or early March. The leaves stay close to the ground, while stems thrust up, bearing as many as six flowers each. As I set the bulbs in the earth near the new row of daffodils, I imagine the doldrums of late winter being given a floral promise of blue skies to come.

⚜ HELLEBORES

It's Virgil who sends me to the hellebores. He mentions them as a component of an ointment to be applied to sheep suffering from skin diseases. The ointment comprises "olive oil lees mixed with silver slag, sulphur, pitch from Mount Ida, wax rich in oil, sea-squill, as well, and strong hellebore and black bitumen." The stuff sounds as if it would be strong enough to do a sheep in rather than cure it. All the ingredients but one were familiar to me. *What* on earth is hellebore? The word was new to me. The answer came from the back page of a garden catalogue that I'd certainly scanned but did not really see—until Virgil prompted me to notice the word printed in bold-face at the upper right of the page. Oh, Lenten roses! The word "hellebore" is simply an anglicization of the Latin *helleborus*. And the plant, a member of the Ranunculaceae, the Buttercup family, is native to Eurasia, as are other members of its genus, *H. niger*, the Christmas rose, and *H. foetida*, "stinking hellebore," which is said to smell somewhat skunky. I have my heart set on *H. orientalis*, "eastern hellebore." What colors it may have sported in its earliest incarnations, I do not know, but today, through cross-breeding and hybridization, the petal-like sepals of the two-inch flowers come in myriad colors, from white and yellow to pink and midnight purple. Some blossoms sport variegations—pink polka-dotted with red, magenta scribbled on white, off-white tinged with green and veined with rose. The leaves are dark and evergreen. I order a strain called 'Royal Heritage' and dig more holes in the terrace. When the plants arrive, their stout roots poke abundantly through the ventilation holes of their plastic pots. Those roots clutch the pots so tightly that they are the very devil to coax loose, but coaxed they are. I set the plants into the holes and pack earth gently around them. Most likely, they'll bloom earlier than Lent and keep blooming for another two months. There's no way to predict their colors. Another set of surprises awaits me.

⚜ FRITILLARIES

I know precisely what colors the fritillaries will be—a bold yellow and an even bolder red. Their binomials make boast of this: *F. imperialis lutea maxima* and *F. imperialis rubra maxima* mean, respectively, "great big yellow imperial fritillary" and "great big red imperial fritillary." Both bear the common name of crown imperial, which speaks to the large and spiky green topknot that they wear; the large, bell-like flowers below may be compared to crowned heads. The flowers are malodorous. One garden writer says, "It's a bit of a puzzle to see them in the elaborate vase paintings of old masters, as when they're cut, their musky odor accompanies them indoors." I doubt that their smell will trouble me, for they shall stay right where they're planted, growing to a height of three feet near the back of the terrace. The same writer, lamenting her failure to grow them happily, calls them "an expensive here-today-gone-tomorrow guest in the garden." I'll give them a try, however. Trying is an integral part of garden dreaming. And next year, they shall be joined, bloom or not, by a kissing cousin, *F. meleagris*, which means "guinea-fowl fritillary." Its delicately checkered blossoms do indeed resemble the subtle patterns of those birds. The only reason that I didn't plant this

more modest species with the other two—it grows to only ten or
twelve inches—is that the nursery was out of stock.

It's fun to think about these members of the Liliaceae, the Lily
family, and, in particular, about *F. meleagris,* for stories reside within
the names. In the chapter of the *Herball* called "Of Turkie or Ginny-
hen Floure," John Gerard describes and illustrates four kinds of fritillaries—the Chequered Daffodill, the Changeable Chequered
Daffodil, the lesser darke yellow Fritillarie, and the early white Fritillarie, and he briefly lists nine others. He also gives a version of the
reason for calling these flowers fritillaries:

> It hath been called *Fritillaria,* of the table or boord upon which
> men play at Chesse, which square checkers the floure doth very
> much resemble; some thinking that it [the chess board] was named
> *Fritillus:* whereof there is no certaintie; for Martialis seemeth to call
> *Fritillus, Abacus,* or the Tables whereat men play at Dice.

The Roman poet Martial (c. A.D. 40–103), mentioned above, gives
the truth. The Latin name for a dice box is *fritillus,* and it would follow that the box was ornamented with a checkered design. The name
refers to the flower's markings, not to its shape.

As for *meleagris,* the Greek species-name deserves a paragraph of
its very own. It denotes a bird. Today, it's the genus-name for the wild
turkey, *Meleagris gallopavo,* but turkeys, native to the Americas, were
unknown in ancient Greece. Turkeys were also unknown to the early
European explorers who traipsed, sometimes encumbered by their
armor, through the New World. Lacking a proper name for the birds
but recognizing them as something in the line of poultry, they gave
them the name properly belonging to guinea fowl. But how did *meleagris* attach itself to guinea fowl? It seems that once upon a time out
of time in Greece, in the days of gods and heroes, a baby, named Meleager, was born to Oeneus, the king of Calydon, and his wife Althaea.
When he was only seven days old, the Fates came to Althaea and said
that the child would live only if a certain stick that lay upon the
hearth was left unburned. Mealager grew to be a famous athlete and

fighter, and he might be alive to this very day if a sin of omission on his father's part had not occured. It seems that Oeneus overlooked the goddess Artemis in his annual sacrifices to the Olympian gods. Artemis, properly incensed, sent an enormous boar to kill Oeneus's farmworkers and cattle and to uproot his crops. Lured by a promise of the boar's skin and tusks, the heroic figures of Greece, including Jason, Castor, and Pollux, rallied, and Atalanta, a swift and successful huntress, joined them. Drawn to Atalanta (though he was married), Meleager quashed the quibbling about allowing a woman to hunt with them, and off they went. It was Meleager who drove home the spear that killed the boar. He thereupon skinned the animal and took its tusks, which he presented to Atalanta. Some of his male cousins began to argue that they, his kin, deserved the trophies. Talk led to blows, and Meleager slew his cousins. As Althaea watched the corpses of her nephews being carried home, the Fates returned and told her to burn the stick that had kept her son alive. Althaea straightway tossed it on the fire. Internecine warfare ensued, and Meleager was easily dispatched. At that, his sisters, the Meleagrides, erupted with ear-piercing ululations. Artemis promptly turned them into guinea fowl, which shriek to this day. Gerard's "Ginny-hen floure" is known by other names—checkerboards and mission bells, for two—but I'll always think of them as the flower representing Meleager's sisters.

Early November: This year's assortment of bulbs is in the earth. The fall crops of broccoli and cauliflower have ripened; a winter's worth of both is in the freezer. As I was standing in the front yard getting ready to harvest the cauli curds, a woman walking by on the other side of the street called out, "What are those big leaves like elephant ears?" I said that I was growing elephants, of course, and invited her to come over for a look. She looked amid the huge gray-green leaves, saw the large white pearls within, and made the proper murmurs of approval. She also illustrates a condition commonly found in our times: ignorance of how cauliflower and broccoli grow, of what the plants look like, and how you trim the newly picked heads. For many of us, the only (not so) fresh cauliflower and broccoli that we're familiar with rest, two for four dollars, on supermarket produce counters or else come served, with carrots, bell peppers, and celery, on a platter of crudités that also holds a bowl of ranch-dressing dip.

The bell and hot peppers still produce, the blanket flowers and marigolds still give off a yellow and orange glow like that of hot embers, but black frost will strike soon. I've tilled the vegetable patches in back, covered them this year with cardboard, and moved the wheeled trash bin to the front so that it's handy for the disposal of frost-bitten plants.

Mid-November: We haven't had a hard freeze yet, but the nights have been cold enough to nip the peppers. Autumn's headlong rush toward winter is palpable. I pick the last of the sweet type, put the leaves and woody trunk into the trash bin, and hope that a few more cayennes will turn red before the two plants in the front yard must be pulled up. Those in the back are already gone. It's time now to empty the tiller of gas and see that the tools are cleaned and stored, their blades coated lightly with oil. One garden writer says of this season, "Our revels now are ended." On the surface, it might seem that way, but, down deep, she's wrong. The giddiness, the flood of pleasure is yet to come. Praise be that Thanksgiving and Christmas are on the way, both to be celebrated with good food from the garden. If not for the merry diversions that holidays provide, I'd be as itchy as a child waiting for Santa, except that my restlessness stems from anticipating the January tide of catalogues—catalogues for seeds, plants, tools, and books. And the thought of catalogues leads to a precept:

Save all the garden catalogues that come your way. Put them on a shelf or in a drawer. Then, use them as reference books, consulting them for information on such matters as colors, varieties, plant-hardiness zones, scientific names, and tips on cultivation.

The seed catalogues begin to arrive the day after Christmas. Because of them, I feel no letdown from the holidays, for January is the month in which daydreams blossom. No cucumber beetles and two-lined spittlebugs, no fungal wilt or thievish squirrels infest the bright pages. I plant the perfect garden, even though it flourishes only in the intensely vivid Technicolor of my imagination. The terrace becomes home to at least two azaleas, one pink, the other orange, and to the coppery gold fern called *Dryopteris erythrosora* ("wood fern with red spore cases"). Orange coneflowers, *Echinacea paradoxa* ("unexpected hedgehog flower," for the prickles of the receptacle) grow and bloom in front of the volunteer redbud. Scarlet runner beans, *Phaseolus coccineus* ("scarlet bean") climb a trellis that already waits for them in a box on the back porch. What reality will bring, I do not know, but looking forward to light from the bleak depths of January is a joyful experience.

Catalogues offering seeds, bulbs, and plants are not the only winter-time prods to the imagination. Two other kinds of catalogue entice—several that feature tools and two that focus on books. At this point in my life, I have almost every tool, from tiller to trowel to pruning hook, that is needed to tend my gardens. But, used for keeping chaos at bay, they are necessities. Catalogues, however, bring visions of the possible. Mind's eye sees a solar-powered fountain with water cascading from a pitcher at the top into a series of bowls. From the bottom, the water is pumped back up to the top. Which would suit the backyard better: terracotta or copper? An adapter for indoor use during winter days may be bought for either model. Solar lights also catch my fancy—but where to put them? Then, self-watering planters beckon. Three or four would make for an undemanding container garden of patio tomatoes and bell peppers. I've already admitted succumbing to the irresistible: a circular, three-tiered strawberry bed, to which a hose may be attached to create a fine spray descending on all below from the top tier. It shall be placed over the spot in the lower backyard that marks the site of the demolished cistern. The ground has sunk a good six inches into the hole: I've stepped down unexpectedly and tripped. The hole could be filled with earth from the terrace, but it makes more sense to convert the hole into a special strawberry garden.

January brings more than catalogues. It brings a precept:

January is the month to start regular peeks outside at the garden. And keep peeking throughout the winter (unless deep snow covers everything).

As surely as the sun rises every morning, green will begin to show itself—the tips of slender daffodil and summer snowflake leaves, little gray-green nubbles where there will be sedum, and fresh blades of chives (not to mention the inescapable wild garlic, the whorled rosettes of daisy fleabane, and winter cress in bloom).

January also brings the seeds that I've ordered. The plain little three-by-four-inch packets arrive. I shake them envisioning their contents: lettuce and carrot seeds like not-quite-finely ground black pepper, radishes like miniature BB-gun pellets, beans kidney-shaped and hefty, the small white Frisbees of the *Capsicums*, the little spears of the marigolds, the zinnias' flat gray ovals. The plump black or black-and-gray-striped sunflower seeds are truly magical: their teardrop shape is that of the ancient Greek symbol for *sun* and *gold*. I imagine their sprouting, the first green stems arching out of starter pots, then lifting their primary leaves. In mind's eye, flowers bloom, fruit is set.

Nor, in winter, can I ignore the books with which publishers tempt me. Two catalogues possess special allure—one is practical, the other scientific. (The lyrical variety of garden book won't be found in any one catalogue. It includes the books of Elizabeth Lawrence and essay collections by Diane Ackerman and Dominique Browning. All whet my thirst for experimentation, for casting off preconceptions and setting in, say, a jungle of elephant ears, tall cannas, and persimmons. Best go to the library or the Internet for them.) Two book catalogues always lead me on. One, strictly of the down-to-earth variety, is Storey Publishing, which issues a series of slender booklets called Country Wisdom Bulletins. They cover matters from growing herbs, peppers, and berries (including strawberries, yes!) to making pickles and flavored vinegars. And Storey publishes regular, multipage books dealing with garden activities from design to composting.

The publisher that has most often caused me to open my purse is The Timber Press, situated in Portland, Oregon. What plants would you like to know more about—daylilies, peonies, ferns, ornamental grasses, cacti? Would you like to build and plant a rock garden or a water garden? How about making a garden of native wildflowers or encouraging a meadow? And what about growing a garden on a hard surface—a rock, a table, or pavement? The instructions are here. Timber issues books on planting a green roof and EC gardening—ecologically correct, that is. Would you like to go farther afield and know more about the vegetation of Japan or the orchids of the Philippines? Timber is your source. History is here, as well, with looks at Native American ethnobotany, not to mention tales of the modern plant-hunters who follow in their predecessors' footsteps all over the world. Timber has also reprinted the lively garden essays of Beverley Nichols (1898–1983), an Englishman who wrote with great (if occasionally gynephobic) élan about the ever-changing plantings at his home, Merry Hall. And, anyone who has read this far and suffered bollixing by an overabundance of scientific nomenclature may blame Timber Press. What would I do without its books explaining the meanings of the binomials?

If you want to know the sources of all these good things, from seeds to tools to books, I shall not leave you in the lurch.

Please consult the appendix for a list of my favorite companies, along with their addresses, phone numbers, and Web sites.

Some gardens, like that of Thomas Jefferson at Monticello, are now living museums, maintained to let present-day visitors appreciate the artistry of the past. But gardens like mine are never finished. They always retain the plasticity of raw clay, for they may be molded and shaped ad infinitum. And that's what winter brings—the chance to make the old new again. Death and resurrection—the eternal cycle is present and immediate in every garden, be it planted centuries ago or just last summer.

Garden dreaming has become important as I age. I'm now in my eighth decade but still finding the energy to take an active role in all the garden tasks. I envision more perennials—a low-maintenance backyard of daylilies, Asiatic lilies, coneflowers, and flowering shrubs. There shall always be some annuals—zinnias, marigolds, sunflowers, and tomatoes, especially tomatoes. My hope is that more and more people will come to understand the complete superiority of Total Garden over Lawn.

May your own garden dreaming be bright and bountiful.

SOURCES FOR ALL GARDENERS

Reliable Favorites

SUNFLOWERS

❧ SEEDS: FLOWER AND VEGETABLE

The Cook's Garden
P. O. Box 535
Londonderry, VT 05148-0535
1-800-457-9703
www.cooksgarden.com

Johnny's Selected Seeds
955 Benton Avenue
Winslow, ME 04901
1-800-879-2258
www.johnnyseeds.com

John Scheepers Kitchen Garden Seeds
P.O. Box 638
Bantam, CT 06750-0638
1-860-567-6086
www.kitchengardenseeds.com

Park's Seeds
1 Parkton Avenue
Greenwood, SC 29647-0001
1-800-845-3369
www.parkseed.com

Totally Tomatoes
Catalog Fulfillment Center
335 South High Street
Randolph, WI 53956
1-803-663-0016
www.totallytomatoes.com

W. Atlee Burpee & Co.
Warminster, PA 18974
1-800-888-1447
www.burpee.com

⚘ BULBS

Dutch Gardens
U.S. Reservation Center
144 Intervale Road
Burlington, VT 05401
1-800-944-2250
www.dutchgardens.com

John Scheepers, Inc.
P. O. Box 638
Bantam, CT 06750-0638
1-860-567-0838
www.johnscheepers.com

White Flower Farm
P. O. Box 50
Litchfield, CT 06759-0050
1-800-503-9624
www.whiteflowerfarm.com

✵ PLANTS: FLOWERS, SHRUBS, AND TREES

Edible Landscaping
361 Spirit Ridge Lane
Afton, VA 22920
1-800-524-4156
www.ediblelandscaping.com

Wayside Gardens
1 Garden Lane
Hodges, SC 29695-0001
1-800-845-1124
www.waysidegardens.com

TOOLS

Charley's Greenhouse & Garden
17979 State Route 536
Mount Vernon, WA 98273-3269
1-800-322-4707
www.charleysgreenhouse.com

Florian
157 Water Street
Southington, CT 06489
1-800-275-3618
www.floriantools.com

Gardener's Supply Company
128 Intervale Road
Burlington, VT 05401
1-800-427-3363
www.gardeners.com

❧ BOOKS

Storey Books
210 MASS MoCA Way
North Adams, MA 01247
www.storey.com

Timber Press, Inc.
133 S.W. Second Avenue, Suite 450
Portland, OR 97204-3527
1-800-327-5680
www.timberpress.com

⚜ NOTES

"Tomato Haven"
Page   1   Tomatoes are good poetry: Dove, 24.

"The Grass Extermination Project"
Page 11   And, as it works: Quiller-Couch, 404.
     11   "Contact with the brown earth": Shirley Hibbard, quoted by Jenny Uglow, 197.
     19   "Rethinking the Lawn": Quammen, 171–180.
     20   "This grazing system": Waddington, 3–4.
     21   "Thorough-Views": *Oxford English Dictionary.*
     22   "for the purpose": BBC Homepage History.
     24   "An estimate made in 1996": Yaling, 930.
     24   "Advertising, mass marketing": Jenkins, 6.
     24   Virginia alone: National Agricultural Statistics Service, 68.
     25   An article: Yaling, 935.
     26   "quality of life": Beard, 453.
     27   "turfgrass surfaces": Beard, 455.
     27   It's been proposed: Hiss, citing studies by John H. Falk, 36–38.

"Tools of the Trade"
Page 31   Once the relation between poetry: Lawrence, quoted by Wilson, 30.
     32   "A man should never wash": Lattimore, 107.
     34   Perhaps I should also sing: Virgil, *Georgics*, Book 4, 119–24.
     35   Unless you pursue: Virgil, *Georgics*, Book 1, 155–59.
     36   Need I mention him: Virgil, *Georgics*, Book 1, 104–110.
     38   that prescribed by the Rodale Press's *Garden Answers*: Bradley, 9.
     38   "A heavy soil": Virgil, *Georgics*, Book 2, 254–55.

39   "muscats from Rhodes," "native grapes": Virgil, *Georgics*, Book 2, 101–2.

46   "They address calcium deficiencies": Stewart, 24.

46   "The earliest references": Campbell, 36.

48   "a bed of hot and new horse dung": Gerard, 909.

50   One calls for beginning: www.rebeccasgarden.com/howto/items/98colda1.html

50   The second plan: www.gardengatemagazine.com/tips/25tip9.html.

53   I've found a drawing: Campbell, 39.

53   "militant farmers' weapons": Virgil, *Georgics*, Book 1, 160.

"How a Garden Grows"

Page 55   No one gardens alone: Lawrence, 5.

58   "Never thank anyone": Hoke, 115.

64   "Are you cruel enough": Lawrence, quoted by Wilson, 238.

64   "It is troubling": Kenyon, 48.

65   "Death & Being": Beam, 17.

65   "The Red-Bud-Tree": Lawson, 106.

67   By mid-century: Haughton, 189–90.

68   "Where no other green thing": Haughton, 190.

"Herbs"

Page 74   Organy given in wine: Gerard, 667.

74   "The plant as it grows wild": Stobart, 185.

75   "Sage is singular good": Gerard, 766.

76   John Gerard credits it: Gerard, 577.

77   "is spice"; "comfort the heart"; "Rosemarie is a remedy": Gerard, 1293–94.

78   Let green and fragrant laurel: Virgil, *Georgics*, Book 4, 30–31

78   "thyme-scented honey": Virgil, *Georgics*, Book 4, 169.

79   "fearefull, melancholike": Gerard, 574.

80   It's said: Lust, 156.

80   "long and fibrous": Gerard, 249.

80 One usually authoritative: Katzer.
81 The Roman naturalist Pliny: Kowalchik and Hylton, 482.
81 "*Ruellius* and such others": Gerard, 249.
82 "the smell of Basill"; "*Dioscorides* saith": Gerard, 674.
84 "must remain the junior partner": Kowalchik and Hylton, 54.

"Flowers"
Page 87 Some garden plants: McIntyre, 33.
90, 91 "Orenge tawny colour"; this plant bringeth forth; "fine and rare plants": Gerard, 98–99.
94 "unpleasant smell"; did see a boy; "these plants": Gerard, 750–51.
94 Scientific research: Dover and others.
95 Another study has shown: Sturz and Kimpinski.
95 One book on edible flowers: Creasy, 48.
97 I've seen an account: Haughton, 435.
99 "sphere whose center": Liddell and Scott, 983.
105 studies have shown: Romero-Romero.
106 The Aztecs: Grieve, 783.
107 "The Indian Sun": Gerard, 751.
107 "exceedingly pleasant meat: Gerard, 752.

"The Secrets of the Vegetables"
Page 111 The vegetables are taking over: Field, 294–95.
112 "The Beane is windie meat": Gerard, 1210.
116 Virgil mentions: Virgil, *Georgics*, Book 4, 130–31.
116 The poet also advises: Virgil, *Georgics*, Book 2, 299.
118 Companion Planting Chart: Kuepper, 2.
121 Sweet Pickle Chips: adapted from Landau, 109.
123 "ranke and stinking savour," "The Apple of Love": Gerard, 346.
126 "hath many large leaves": Gerard, 314.
126 "preserve a man," "the bitings of venemous beasts": Gerard, 317.

131   "serveth love matters"; "containeth in it": Gerard, 1029.
132   Carrot Marmalade: adapted from Landau, 67.
135   "chiles are often referred to": Katzer.
136   Ginnie pepper: Gerard, 365.
138   "a habit worth acquiring": Schweid, 141.

"Outwitting the Gardener"
Page143   Everywhere the best ornamental grounds: Olmsted,
        quoted by Larson, 172.
144   Citing not only; Boiled, it strengthens: Gerard, 290–91.
145   "There was a reason for this": Haughton, 105.
145   What Man named: Beam, 34.
146   Haymaids, Hedgemaids": Grieve, 442.
146   Ale-hoofe, Gill go by ground; "tunned up in ale"; "com-
        mended against": Gerard, 856–57.
149   "by reason of his fierie": Gerard, 888.
149   Biting Clematis, white Clematis: Gerard, 890.
149   British book on flower fairies; "a shady bower": Warne,
        next to last page.
153   "without tearing up": Pinto, 110.
154   The leaves of Mallowes: Gerard, 932.
155   "Henbit" and "Henne-bit"; "bastard Chickweeds"; "dead
        Nettell"; "slender blew floures": Gerard, 615–17.
155   "If you happen to have": Schwartz.

"Wooing the Green Man, Courting Dame Kind"
Page161   "The advocate of cultivation": Ross, 8–9.
161   "scale, proportion": Alice Recknagel Ireys, quoted by
        Ross, 151.
164   Father of Wine-Making: Virgil, *Georgics*, Book 2, 4–8.
164   When Arcturus rises . . . barley in the fields.: Virgil,
        Georgics, Book 1, 68–69; 208–11; and 219–24, respectively.
173   "The sap yields": Coues, quoted by Peattie, 474.

"Garden Dreaming"
Page 185 Gardening is the slowest moving: Miller, quoted in Deitz, 31.
187 "The common yellow Daffodill"; "But as for body"; "being stamped"; Gerard, 132.
188 "Winter Wolfes-bane"; "Whole leaves come forth of the ground": Gerard, 967.
189 "The delightful thing"; "faint underlying tinge": Lawrence, 39.
189 "olive oil lees": Virgil, *Georgics*, Book 3, 448–51.
190 "It's a bit of a puzzle"; "an expensive here-today-gone-to-morrow": McIntyre, 144.
191 It hath been called: Gerard, 151.
193 "Our revels": Kenyon, 43.

✢ BIBLIOGRAPHY

Ackerman, Diane. *Cultivating Desire: A Natural History of My Garden.* New York: HarperCollins Publishers, Inc., 2001.

Agricultural Research Service, United States Department of Agriculture. *Common Weeds of the United States.* New York: Dover Publications, 1971. Republication of *Selected Weeds of the United States* first issued by the United States Department of Agriculture (Gov't Printing Office), 1970.

Barker, Cicely Mary. *The Flower Fairies Changing Seasons.* Harmondsworth, Middlesex, England: Frederick Warne, 1992.

BBC Home History. [Internet] Available from: http:/www.bbc.co.uk/history/ historic_figures/budding_edwin_beard.shtml.

Beam, Jeffery. *Visions of Dame Kind.* Winston-Salem, North Carolina: The Jargon Society, 1995.

Beard, James B., and Robert L. Green. "The Role of Turfgrasses in Environmental Protection and Their Benefits to Humans," *Journal of Environmental Quality*, Vol. 23, No. 3 (May–June 1994), pages 452–60.

Betts, Edwin Morris. *Thomas Jefferson's Garden Book, 1766–1824.* Philadelphia: The American Philosophical Society, 1992.

Betts, Janice Lake, and Wendell G. Mathews, eds. *Turfgrass: Nature's Constant Benediction, The History of the American Sod Producers Association, 1967–1992.* Rolling Meadows, IL: The American Sod Producers Association, 1992.

Bianchi, Martha Dickinson, and Alfred Leete Hampton, eds. *Poems by Emily Dickinson.* Boston: Little, Brown and Company, 1957.

Bradley, Fern Marshall, ed. *Garden Answers: At-a-Glance Solutions for Every Gardening Problem.* Emmaus, Pennsylvania: Rodale Press, 1995.

Brown, Lauren. *Grasses: An Identification Guide.* Boston: Houghton Mifflin Company, 1979.

Browning, Dominique. *Paths of Desire: The Passions of a Suburban Gardener.* New York: Scribner, 2004.

Campbell, Susan. *Charleston Kedding: A History of Kitchen Gardening.* London: Trafalgar Square Books, 1996.

Carr, Anna. *Good Neighbors: Companion Planting for Gardeners.* Emmaus, Pennsylvania: Rodale Press, 1985.

———. *Rodale's Color Handbook of Garden Insects.* Emmaus, Pennsylvania: Rodale Press, 1979.

Coombes, Allen J. *Dictionary of Plant Names.* Portland, Oregon: Timber Press, 1994.

Creasy, Rosalind. *The Edible Flower Garden.* Boston, Massachusetts: Periplus Editions (HK) Ltd., 1999.

Cunningham, Sally Jean. *Great Garden Companions: A Companion-Planting System for a Beautiful, Chemical-Free Vegetable Garden.* Emmaus, Pennsylvania: Rodale Press, Inc., 1998.

Daniels, Stevie. *The Wild Lawn Handbook: Alternatives to the Traditional Front Lawn.* New York: Macmillan, 1995.

Deitz, Paula. "A Gardener for the People," *Smith Alumnae Quarterly,* Vol. 91, No. 1 (Fall 2004), pp. 26–31.

Dove, Rita. *The Yellow House on the Corner.* Pittsburgh: Carnegie Mellon University Press, 1989.

Dover, K. E., R. McSorley, and K.-H Wang. "Marigolds as Cover Crops." [Internet] Available from: http://agroecology.ifas,uft.edu/marigoldsbackgroundd.htm

Dunmire, William W. *Gardens of New Spain: How Mediterranean Plants and Foods Changed America.* Austin: University of Texas Press, 2004.

Fairy Encyclopedia. [Internet] Available from: www.geocities.com/ahtens/Forum/4611/fairyD.html

Farallones Institute. *The Integral Urban House: Self-Reliant Living in the City.* San Francisco: Sierra Club Books, 1979.

Field, Edward, ed. *A Geography of Poets.* New York: Bantam Books Inc., 1979.

Gerard, John. *The Herball, or Generall Historie of Plantes.* The Complete 1633 Edition as Revised and Enlarged by Thomas

Johnson. New York: Dover Publications, Inc., 1975. An unabridged replication of the work originally published by Adam Islip, Joice Norton and Richard Whitakers, London, 1633.

Grieve, Mrs. M. *A Modern Herbal: The Medicinal, Culinary, Cosmetic and Economic Properties, Cultivation and Folk-Lore of Herbs, Grasses, Fungi, Shrubs & Trees with All Their Modern Scientific Uses.* 2 vols. New York: Dover Publications, Inc., 1971. Reprint of a work originally published by Harcourt, Brace & Company, 1931.

Haughton, Claire Shaver. *Green Immigrants: The Plants That Transformed America.* New York: Harcourt Brace Jovanovitch, 1978.

Hicks, Clive. *The Green Man: A Field Guide.* Helhoughton, England: *Compassbooks,* 2000.

Hiss, Tony. *The Experience of Place.* New York: A. A. Knopf, 1990.

Hoke, N. C. "Folk-Custom and Folk-Belief in North Carolina," *The Journal of American Folklore,* Vol. 5, No. 17 (April–June 1892), pages 113–120.

James, Alice. "Worm Composting: Vermiculture," Texas Natural Resource Conservation Commission, 1995. [Internet] Available from: www.tnrcc.state.tx.us/exec/sbea/tes/lessons99/vermiculture.html.

Jenkins, Virginia Scott. *The Lawn: A History of an American Obsession.* Washington and London: Smithsonian Institution Press, 1994.

Katzer, Gernot. "Gernot Katzer's Spice Pages." [Internet] Available from: www.ang.kfunigraz.ac.at/~katzer/engl/generic_frame.html?caps_fru.html.

Kenyon, Jane. *A Hundred White Daffodils.* Saint Paul, Minnesota: Graywolf Press, 1999.

Kowalchik, Claire, and William H. Hylton, eds. *Rodale's Illustrated Encyclopedia of Herbs.* Emmaus, Pennsylvania: Rodale Press, 1987.

Kuepper, George, and Mardi Dodson. "Companion Planting: Basic Concepts and Resources," July, 2001. [Internet] Available from: www.attra.org/attra-pub/complant.html.

Landau, Lois M., and Laura G. Myers. *Too Many Tomatoes, Squash, Beans, and Other Good Things: A Cookbook for When Your Garden Explodes.* New York: HarperPerennial, 1991.

Larson, Erik. *The Devil in the White City: Murder, Magic, and Madness at the Fair That Changed America.* New York: Crown Publishers, 2003.

Lattimore, Richmond, translator. *Hesiod.* Ann Arbor: The University of Michigan Press, 1959.

Lawrence, Elizabeth. *A Southern Garden.* Chapel Hill and London: University of North Carolina Press, 1991.

———. *The Little Bulbs: A Tale of Two Gardens.* Durham: Duke University Press, 1986.

Lawson, John. *A New Voyage to Carolina.* Edited by Hugh Talmage Lefler. Chapel Hill: The University of North Carolina Press, 1967.

Lembke, Janet. *Touching Earth: Reflections on the Restorative Power of Gardening.* Short Hills, NJ: Burford Books, 2001.

Lust, John. *The Herb Book.* New York: Bantam Books, 1974.

Martin, Alexander C. *Weeds.* Racine, Wisconsin: Western Publishing Company, Inc., 1972.

Matthews, John. *The Green Man: Spirit of Nature.* Boston, Massachusetts: Red Wheel, 2002.

McIntire, Suzanne. *An American Cutting Garden: A Primer for Growing Cut Flowers Where Summers Are Hot and Winters Are Cold.* Charlottesville and London: University Press of Virginia, 2002.

Millspaugh, Charles F. *American Medicinal Plants.* New York: Dover Publications, Inc., 1974. Reprint of *Medicinal Plants*, published by John C. Yorston & Company, Philadelphia, 1892.

National Agricultural Statistics Service. *Virginia's Turfgrass Industry: A Report Covering Home Lawns, Highway Roadsides, Parks, General Areas, Golf Courses, Sod Farms, Service Companies, Cemeteries, Churches, Schools, Airports.* Richmond, Virginia: May, 2000.

National Gardening Association. *Dictionary of Horticulture*. New
    York: Penguin Books, 1994.
North Dakota State University. "Sunflower Production." [Internet]
    Available from:
    www.ext.nodak.edu/extpubs/plantsci/rowcrops/eb25w-3.htm.
Ondra, Nancy and Linda Hager. *Weed-Ending Secrets: What Weeds
    Don't Want You to Know*. Emmaus, Pennsylvania: Rodale Press,
    Inc., 1994.
Ortho Books. *The Garden That Cares for Itself*. San Ramon, CA:
    The Solaris Group, 1990.
Peattie, Donald Culross. *A Natural History of Trees: Of Eastern and
    Central North America*. Boston: Houghton Mifflin Company,
    1966.
Peterson, Roger Tory, and Margaret McKenny. *A Field Guide to
    Wildflowers of Northeastern and North-Central North America*.
    Boston: Houghton Mifflin Company, 1968.
Pinto, Vivian de Sola, ed. *William Blake*. New York: Schocken
    Books, 1965.
Quammen, David. *The Boilerplate Rhino: Nature in the Eye of the
    Beholder*. New York: Scribner, 2000.
Quiller-Couch, Sir Arthur, ed. *The Oxford Book of English Verse,
    1250–1918*. London: Oxford University Press.
Riotte, Louise. *Carrots Love Tomatoes: Secrets of Companion Plant-
    ing for Successful Gardening*. North Adams, Massachusetts:
    Storey Publishing, 1998.
Romero-Romero, Teresa, Ana Luisa Anaya, and Rocio Cruz-Ortega.
    "Screening for Effects of Phytochemical Variability on Cyto-
    plasmic Protein Synthesis of Crop Plants," *Journal of Chemical
    Ecology*, Vol. 28, No. 3 (March, 2002), pp. 617–29.
Ross, Stephanie. *What Gardens Mean*. Chicago and London: The
    University of Chicago Press, 1998.
Sargent, Charles Sprague. *Manual of the Trees of North America*. 2
    vols. New York: Dover Publications, Inc., 1965. An unabridged
    and unaltered republication of the second (1922) edition of

the work originally published by Houghton Mifflin Company in 1905.

Schweid, Richard. *Hot Peppers: The Story of Cajuns & Capsicum*. Rev. ed. Chapel Hill & London: University of North Carolina Press, 1999.

Sherman, Rhonda. Private correspondence.

Smith, A. W. *A Gardener's Handbook of Plant Names: Their Meanings and Origins*. Mineola, New York: Dover Publications, Inc., 1997. An unabridged republication of *A Gardener's Handbook of Plant Names*, Harper & Row, 1963.

Stewart, Amy. *The Earth Moved: On the Remarkable Achievements of Earthworms*. Chapel Hill: Algonquin Books, 2004.

Stobart, Tom. *Herbs, Spices and Flavorings*. Harmondsworth, Middlesex, England: Penguin Books, 1977.

Sturz, A. V., and J. Kimpinski. "Endroot bacteria derived from marigolds (*Tagetes* spp.) can decrease soil population densities of root-lesion nematodes in the potato root zone," *Plant and Soil*, 2004, pp. 241–249.

Sullivan, Preston. "Overview of Cover Crops and Green Manures: Fundamentals of Sustainable Agriculture," July 2003. [Internet] Available from: www.attra.ncat.org.

Thomas Jefferson Agricultural Institute. "Sunflower: A Native Oilseed with Growing Markets." [Internet] available from: www.jeffersoninstitute.org/pubs/sunflower.shtml.

Timmermann, Annette, ed. *500 Essential Garden Plants*. Köln: DuMont Buchverlag, 2001.

Uglow, Jenny. *A Little History of British Gardening*. New York: North Point Press, 2004.

United States Department of Agriculture. "Nutritive Value of Foods." Home and Garden Bulletin Number 72. Washington, D.C.: U.S. Government Printing Office, 1978.

United States Department of Agriculture. Plants Database. [Internet] Available from: http://plants.usda.gov/index.html.

Virgil. *Georgics*. Translated by Janet Lembke. New Haven and London: Yale University Press, 2005.

Waddington, D. V., R. N. Carrow, and R. C. Sherman, co-editors. *Turfgrass.* Madison, Wisconsin: American Society of Agronomy, Inc., Crop Science Society of America, Inc., Soil Science Society of America, Inc., 1992.

Wasowski, Sally, and Andy Wasowski. *Requiem for a Lawnmower: Gardening in a Warmer, Drier World.* 2nd ed. Lanham: Taylor Publishing Company, 2004.

Wilson, Emily Herring. *No One Gardens Alone: A Life of Elizabeth Lawrence.* Boston: Beacon Press, 2004.

Yaling, Qian, and Ronald F. Follett. "Assessing Soil Carbon Sequestration in Turfgrass Systems Using Long-Term Soil Testing Data." *Agronomy Journal* 94 (2000), 930–935.

✥ INDEX

Tarragon